Cleaved

Sermons of reconciliation in a world of disparity

Christopher M. Tweel

Cleaved: Sermons of reconciliation in a world of disparity
ISBN: Softcover 978-1-955581-27-1
Copyright © 2021 by Christopher M. Tweel

All rights reserved. No part of this book may be reproduced or transmitted in any form or by any means, electronic or mechanical, including photocopying, recording, or by any information storage and retrieval system, without permission in writing from the publisher.

Parson's Porch Books is an imprint of Parson's Porch & Company (PP&C) in Cleveland, Tennessee. PP&C is an innovative organization which raises money by publishing books of noted authors, representing all genres. Its face and voice is **David Russell Tullock** (dtullock@parsonsporch.com).

Parson's Porch & Company *turns books into bread & milk* by sharing its profits with the poor.

www.parsonsporch.com

Cleaved

For Amara and Bailey.
For both Lilys, Juniper, Isaiah, Ezra,
Caleb and Joshua.
For Lucy and Clay.
For Luca and Cora.
For Mira, Lena and Andy.

Be tenacious in the truth and the love you bring to the world.

Contents

Author's Note 9
Pit-ward 15
SuperHeroine 21
Injustice Anywhere 26
It's Woe for Everyone 31
The Cost of Unity 38
Not Just my Feet 43
It's the Un-withered Leaf 48
Jesus Can't Stand the In-Laws Either 52
The Incarcerated Church 57
How the Mighty have Fallen 62
Sabbath as Healing 68
Epigenetic Good News 73
What we leave Behind 78
In the Belly 84
All Things 89
Partnering with the Spirit 95
The Good Thing 102
Anti-Prosperity 106
Perceivable Newness 110
Surrounded by Death 116
Hospitable Ears 122
It's the End of the World 128
The Journey after the Wreck 132
In the Time of Wrath 136

Author's Note

Since 2016 the focus of many pastors, authors and justice workers has been the fight against a newly apparent racism, misogyny and fear-mongering in the United States. It seemed that for many the veneer of civility had been torn away and, for the better possibly, we were all exposed to one another. This inevitably led to a lot of division in our churches, in our families, our schools -- everywhere. Again, this was possibly a good thing. Throughout this era, I've had the honor to bear witness to a church whose hearts' were torn. Politically, morally, and economically many of our members found themselves on sides that they saw as opposite. Our calling was to encourage genuine healing that did not negate the work -- the real spiritual work -- of anti-racism that many people were being encouraged to assume by the Holy Spirit.

Seeing one another as enemies is easy.

At times, I admit I desperately wanted to do this. There are people who arguably "deserve" to be treated as enemies. People who try very hard to create walls and conflict wherever they go under the guise of righteousness. People who are legitimately dangerous because of their lifestyle of hate. The harder path is to find a way forward together, while desperately calling those who cause harm to come with us, even as we recognize how we participate in that same harm and seek to undo it. Even as we prudently protect ourselves.

We are called to unity, yet, there is a very real evil that is present in our world. The slaveholders of old had their own religion that was not righteous or reflective of anything that the Bible is actually about. There is truly a new heresy that has taken hold of some in the United States, and it is a destructive power in the world. Yet, as Rev. Dr. William J. Barber is fond of saying "we have to *produce* truth and love." That is our charge. That is our mandate. That is how we combat real evil.

So, the true Christian stands at a confluence of urgencies. As God described in the book of Amos, we are required to engage with and unmake the evil of this world where we find it. The new gods of false patriotism, division and fear of the "other" run in the same vein that led God's strong admonition of Israel's lack of care for the poor, and the profit they make from the vulnerable. We stand now in a time of God's prophecy to Amos coming true. The people of God wander from shore to shore looking for God's word but who cannot find or hear it. In the midst of that, we are responsible for bringing the Good News to the world, and bearing witness to the real power of God through Jesus Christ against the powerful and wealthy idolaters and heretics.

It's a tall order. My hope is that this collection of sermons is at least a start along that path. I am still learning and gathering my understanding of how the Christian can be most purposefully useful in the world, and I too struggle against the desire to cut off the people who create harm and trauma in my community, as opposed to finding a way to love them.

I was sorely tempted to do this while I participated in Charlottesville's now-famous rally in 2017.

The clergy, after the initial stance against the racists rallying in the parks of the city, dispersed to several smaller areas, and many gathered at First United Methodist which was a staging area and welcome center for all people of faith and peace during the rally. The church sits directly across from the Market Street park where the statue of racist rebellion leader Robert Lee stands (for now). The clergy made the rounds as other protesters came in. We met with people as they parked and came to the early morning meeting place. We organized snacks and water. We reviewed emergency plans and procedures. The church in Charlottesville operated that day as a place for people who were present for peace, so many of the Alt-Right demonstrators were refused entry as they carried assault rifles and handguns.

To be clear, I grew up with firearms, and so their presence, which told a story as to the intentions of the Alt-Right and their need to intimidate, did not bother me *per se*. Instead, it was the growling vitriol that was wound into their faces as they passed by. It was the look of hate that rankled me as clergy were called "Race-traitors," and worse. As priests and pastors were spit on and cursed.

Later in the day, I was handing out water in the back parking lot and watching as various groups walked up and down the roads adjacent to us. It was a pleasant moment, to be honest. It felt like a victory had been won earlier that morning as people of faith stood arm in arm against the people of hate and out sang their vicious cries of hate and fear. We sang of light and love. Their rally in the park was dispersed by the authorities of the city, and things were taking a peaceful turn. We felt good. We felt like we had come together for the greater purpose of God and had seen God's power against real evil.

Then someone near me shouted in quick succession, "Gun, gun, gun!"

I am not tactically trained. I am slow to respond and even slower in crisis situations. Usually, it works in my favor, giving me time and mental space to consider real solutions in a problematic space. Here it could have cost me my life.

About 15 feet from where I was standing, a young guy from the Alt-Right had drawn a handgun and was pointing it at the counter-protesters in the direction of the church and where many of us were gathered. He held it two-handed, combat grip style, and darted nervously with the barrel moving from person to person on the street and along the sidewalk as people scattered. I stood there in a surreal moment of disbelief, and simply thought, "This isn't right."

Then someone grabbed my arm.

The protocol that was previously discussed in our education meetings preceding the rally was that on the occasion that there was a gun drawn on or near church property people would be pulled inside and the church would go into a "lockdown" mode in order to keep as many people as possible as safe as possible. I don't know who it was that grabbed my arm, but it broke my stupor long enough to join the swift flood of folks pouring into the church as the doors were shut and locked by deacons.

As it turned out no shots were fired by the gunman that day.

That wasn't something we knew at the time while hundreds of people -- clergy, protesters and medical teams -- stood in the hallways of the church waiting for a shot to ring out. Many people wondered about others, friends and partners, who might still be outside. Calls of "has anyone seen...?" were passed up and down the mass of people and into classrooms and the sanctuary. People were scared and angry and undone.

The same emotions that would be echoed only a few blocks away only moments later when Heather Heyer was murdered by one of the Alt-Right in his car.

I thought at that moment, "How does the true Christian bring life to this space of death and fear?" This has always been the question: from the days of Amos walking into the northern kingdom of Isreal to pastors who linked arms and walked up to armed Klansmen with murder in their eyes in Charlottesville in 2017.

Over the past few years, I have sought to help others answer that question in a way that reveals our genuineness and still has the ability to create real change in our neighborhoods.

At our best, the Christian can recognize the church's acts of complicity in history that have brought more sin, death, and idolatry in the world. We can admit that the Bible was and still is sometimes used as a tool for harm and that verses have been intentionally weaponized. We can see the long arm of hate that our own government perpetuates.

We can do all of this and still accept our place as fallen people who are new creations with a charge from the Creator of All to bear witness to the good, the "*chesed*" of God, the loving-kindness that is the unending spring of water found in Jesus Christ. I am convinced that there is this path. The path that doesn't let evil in our hearts rest in a shell of complacency, but holds each person accountable to their own call to bring real Truth and real Love.

It is a path that we can only walk together.

Shalom,

One Sunday

there is a palm in gilead
with branches strewn around
the bareness of the trunk
belies the fullness of the crown.

the master entered humbly riding
amongst the honor of the crowd
sharing the weight of the gathered mass
the ass's head is bowed.

the trees
along the street stand stripped
sacrificed, before a king.
the people misunderstanding
what Messiah brings

The palms stand bare
and empty
a trembling shakes their core
all creation vibrates at the rising
of the One who goes before.

1
Pit-ward

Written after the "Unite the Right" rally in Charlottesville, Virginia

ISAIAH 52:7
ROMANS 10:14-21
GENESIS 37:19-25

It seems disingenuous to talk about Good News this morning in the wake of a state of emergency being called on a city barely 60 miles away. Or perhaps it is the only thing we can declare in the face of conflict. Because there is *Good News*; Jesus Christ is our Salvation and our Lord, and Charlottesville will not be broken or cowed by the evil actions of men and women in its streets.

The passage that Paul is quoting in Romans about good news comes from Isaiah 52, which is an invitation for the people of Zion to rejoice and is written for an audience on the brink of chaos and war. The eighth-century readers or listeners of Isaiah were on the brink of conflict and exile from the Babylonians, an incredibly fearsome power, and they were in a constant state of fear. And here the prophet Isaiah is talking about pretty feet.

The folks originally listening to this passage, however, were encouraged by this, as we all can and should be. What they heard was the truth of their past: that they had been slaves before, in Egypt and in Assyria, and that God had carried them through that as a people and that the time would come *again* for joy and freedom. 'Captives,' the passage reads, 'loosen the bond from your neck, and hear the good news of peace coming down from the mountain of the Lord.'

> *How beautiful upon the mountains*
>   *are the feet of the messenger who announces peace,*
> *who brings good news,*
>   *who announces salvation,*

A message that is so good that even the tired, dusty, sweaty feet of the messenger are beautiful. It was meant to bring hope: they would return to a place of peace.

But God's people were preparing for war and surrounded by death and fear.

There is evil in the world. There were vile and evil people in Charlottesville this weekend, waving their flags and chanting their slogans.

People who were, make no mistake, there to fight. They marched the streets with helmets on and home-made shields and batons, and hand-guns that they drew on people, and loaded assault rifles that they carried openly in the streets. How can the folks in Charlottesville hear this messenger with beautiful feet bringing good news in the wake of death and violence? How could the people of Israel hear it in the eighth century? Or Paul's church in Rome? Or our church in Virginia?

Interestingly enough our verse from Genesis also deals with evil people. This text tells us only a part of the story about Joseph and his amazing coat. The dreamer, the prophet, the late-born son of the most prominent Jewish family. Joseph's father was no stranger to brotherly squabbles but ended his own story with his brother Esau on the side of reconciliation after a Godly-rebranding and a lot of soul searching. In Joseph's story, it is very different from his dad's experience.

It's possible that over-familiarity has clouded our resonance with Joseph's plight. Perhaps we have read the story, heard the musical, and seen movies about the story of Joseph so much that our minds skip ahead to the part about him being the right hand of a pharaoh gladly saving two nations from slow death by starvation. Instead of a complete narrative, let's look at it together as a short story in a collection, or a serialized show that ended for the season here with a cliffhanger. Let's imagine that we are people in the eighth-century looking at an invading army being told to be hopeful that we will return from exile. Let's lock arms with clergy in Charlottesville staring into the face of armed gunmen who are shouting their hate for us and flecking our clothes with the spittle of their rage. Let's pretend we don't know how the story is going to end.

That's a scary place.

That's where Joseph is.

And how did things go so wrong for him? At the start of this day in the ancient world, Joseph -- who I imagine as a happy go lucky boy -- was walking out into the world with a spring in his proverbial step, gone out to find his brothers in Shechem. Shechem is a good place. A well-known town. A safe place. Joseph's dad actually built an altar there called *El-elohe-israel*, meaning "God the God of Israel." A sweet way dear old dad had of claiming and announcing that he was a person of God's own.

That's not where the brothers are though. They are twelve miles north in Dothan.

This is where the theme from the movie "Jaws" should start. That subtle musical cue that tells us something bad is lurking where we can't see.

Joseph has no idea though and continues on the 12 miles north to Dothan, a town and surrounding pasture land whose name means "two pits."

The strings start playing in the background; Buh-dum. Buh-dum...

As Joseph nears Dothan, not even having arrived there, his brothers decide that they are going to kill him. "That snivelling little upstart who doesn't know his place. He's not one of us, and he thinks he is better than us. He's taken our jobs and our place in the family that we are entitled to have by rank of birth. Let's kill him. That will put an end to the ridiculous dream that he has."

These are the words of evil people.

They have premeditated the deed and already have a way to dispose of the body and an alibi to exonerate themselves. "No one talks. We are united in this, right?" they say to each other. To help our modern minds understand the deeper significance of murder as if that wasn't enough, Ruben steps in. As the firstborn, Ruben has the most right to be angry with Joseph, but the vile thing that the brothers propose is too vicious and out of line even for him. He comes up with a plan and shares it with his brothers. The thing that convinces him of his idea are the laws outlined by God against the great sin that shedding the blood of your family would be. "Let us not shed his blood,"he says. From there, brother Judah figures out a way to profit from the whole mess, by selling him into slavery, and ruins Ruben's good intentions to save him, perhaps until people have cooled off. Somehow they pulled this off while Ruben was in the restroom or something.

The Hebrew text does something interesting here. It tells us how uncaring these brothers were because they don't exactly throw him *into* the pit, they throw him *towards* the pit. They cast his body in the general direction of the pit, the implication being that he had no power of his own, and was being tossed aside to live or die. Scripture seems oddly eager to tell us that there was no water in the pit. Genesis 37:24 says twice, "...the pit was empty, there was no water in it."

These pits were dug out as wells and cisterns. Seasonally they would fill or empty depending on many factors, which is why having several on hand made sense. You never knew when one was going to run dry. The light did not reach the bottom, which we know from the circumference work of Eratosthanese[1] the mathematician. Even the famous well he used at Syene, Egypt only had light directly into the bottom once a year. The point is that the brothers had no idea if there was water in the well (the pit) or not. Nor did they particularly care. Scripture fills that in for the reader as an aside so that we know he's not yet dead, as the cistern was empty.

These are the actions of evil people.

And then? They had a nice lunch. It's even possible that they were eating the food that Joseph had brought with him from home. This level of terribleness and hate for their own brother was normalized. It bothered them not at all. It was simply a part of their day. They didn't wring their hands or

---

[1] Eratosthenes' "Geography" by Eratosthenes

give him a second thought until they had an idea about how they might profit from it. Aren't these people we could classify as evil? Even Ruben is going along with all this, instead of telling the truth and accepting the consequence. Joseph is sold as a slave to Egypt. A foreign power so large and secure that the end of our short story is telling us we are never going to see Joseph again.

And yet. We know that's not true.

We do see Joseph again -- we see his brothers and what's more, is that we see them reconcile.

That's good news. That's incredible news, unbelievable even. But how on earth do we get there from evil men eating lunch over a body that may or may not be still alive?

To the church in Rome, Paul says that proclaiming our servanthood to Jesus Christ, knowing deep in our heart that Jesus was God in flesh, and understanding that there are no divisions in this living invitation -- this is good news.

Accepting that Jesus is human and divine.

I wish I felt like that was all I really had to do.

At this moment, considering we weep together the day after people were brutalized and one woman was murdered in a town barely an hour away by a new crop of a vile organization we thought long dead? Recognizing the divinity of Christ seems simple compared to living into our Discipleship of Christ and knowing God is here to save and be Savior for every person. Jew or Greek. Slave or Free. Male or female. Killers and victims.

Saying that Christ died for the killers sounds shocking and gross to even say, but we know it to be true.

I can be angry, as angry as I can be about them. I can weep alongside those who have suffered and fight the good fight with them, and still have to pray for the people who have made themselves our enemies. Not just *our* enemies, not just the enemies of humankind the world over, but people who have made themselves the enemies of God - enemies of the mighty and unconquerable power sitting on the throne of heaven.

In Matthew 5:44, the verse which gives us our orders to love the enemy, the word there for an enemy in Greek is (ἐχθρός) *ekthros* meaning "the hateful, the odious," and those who are at enmity with God in their sin. That's who the people spouting hate in Charlottesville are. That's who the Babylonians were. That's our band of brothers who sold Joseph as a slave. Ekthros. Enemies.

We are charged with praying for them. Finding a way to love them.

Not only that, but we are called to bring them the Good News. Because, how will they know if they have never heard? How will they hear if we do not proclaim? Paul asks us these questions. He asks you and me. That's living into our discipleship, into our true Christ following. That is what proclaiming ourselves to be servants of Jesus Christ is. It's not a static word from our lips.

The Greek understanding of proclamation is a constant lived into word that goes on and on throughout one's life. It's not a statement -- it's a mode that takes over.

That is what it takes for me to have good thoughts about the hateful. I have to call upon all of the things that we have internalized about the nature of God and the love with which God placed Jesus here on earth for every human's salvation from everlasting death. That's the only way I can pray for these enemies of ours. That's the only way I can see pictures of odious killers and know that God's good news is here for them too. By calling on the power that spun the universe to life.

When did Joseph pray, do you think? From the bottom of the pit? Half conscious with the taste of blood in his mouth with no light wondering if he would live or die? From the palace? As he watched his brothers, his enemies, come with years of age on them, begging to be fed as they faced starvation for themselves and their households? At some point in that story the enemies, the odious killers became family again. That is nothing short of one of the most powerful miracles in scripture. Because that's what it takes; a miracle.

In Egypt, there was a miracle as Joseph prayed for his brothers who tried to murder him and enslaved him.

In Babylon, there was a miracle as people remembered the words of hope Isaiah gave them and prayed for their captors.

In Charlottesville too, inside the church not 100 yards from the rallying cry of hateful enemies, with its doors open to their anger, we prayed for them. And that feels like a miracle.

"How will they know, unless people are sent to proclaim," Paul asks. How will our enemies know there is another way if we do not proclaim it to them and act it out. How will the evil and violent people of this world, so full of hate and ugly pain that it falls out of their mouths in ways they can barely help -- how will they know if we aren't ready with Good News even for them? That is possibly the hardest thing any of us could ever do. To meet the enemy with God's Love. How can we possibly answer that call?

We can live our lives well. We can find actions that speak to us and participate. We can speak out against microaggressions and subversive racism, and partner with people we don't yet know to change our neighborhoods, and our city. We can challenge ourselves to move out of our protective privilege. We can daily act and thereby proclaim our servanthood to Jesus Christ our Savior. We could allow ourselves to be utterly changed.

There was perhaps another miracle in Charlottesville that I don't believe made it into the news feeds. Early in the morning, the Alt-Right hate groups, Nazis and the KKK started walking to the park. They could be heard as they came, chanting and banging on their shields. A slow drum, the monotone chants of enemies shouting slogans and slowly coming closer. It was meant to induce fear. It was meant to give the world their news of hate.

Then, there was another sound. It was so soft at first, and then it got louder and louder, it was a song. A simple song that we all might know. I could just barely hear it; "This little light of mine, I'm going to let it shine..." It was the faithful. All the gathered believers who were singing together from somewhere across the park, and soon after, the people on the steps of the church picked it up, and then more and more started singing until you couldn't hear the enemy at all. They sang on and on for a good while, inventing verses about love and God's power on the spot, they sang to the enemy and prayed for them. They sang a song that the enemy could not sing. They sang on their behalf about the light of God that is in every person.

What then do we do if our enemy seems too great? If our family seems to have turned on us? If Babylon is at the gate clamoring for war, and we cannot find it in ourselves to utter a prayer or bravely proclaim the good news and the Lordship of Jesus Christ -- then sing. Find just enough courage to sing that simple song to start, and watch how others will take up the tune until the enemy has been drowned out and overwhelmed in it.

2
SuperHeroine

Written after Bree Newsome climbed a flagpole to remove the confederate battle flag from the grounds of the South Carolina statehouse grounds

JUDGES 4:1-24
2 TIMOTHY 1:5-9

For the Fourth of July, our little girl wanted desperately to wear her Wonder Woman outfit, complete with cape. I hesitated a little bit, thinking of family pictures and, whether the more appropriate outfit might be a skirt, but I let her have her way. It's the right color scheme, after all, complete with stars, and as a friend reminded me, Wonder Woman does work in Washington D.C. When she was created in 1942, Wonder Woman, whose secret identity was Diana Prince, was an army nurse and through the years the character has been an astronaut, a staff person at the UN, and even a military intelligence officer.

My daughter, Amara, loves to feel the cape flapping on her back. She loves running down the path full tilt with her fists out, and she is sure to yell back at us, and ask, "Is my cape flapping? Can you see it?"

There is something captivating about the superheroes and heroines.

Since the stage debut of the Scarlet Pimpernel in 1903 (written by Baroness Orczy), and the comic book explosion of characters in the late 1930s, our culture has always made a place for these stories, of heroes and heroines. Batman and Superman. Scarlet Witch and Captain Marvel. They are in our movies, our T.V shows and countless books and comics. As I read through today's verse in Judges, I saw why.

The story of Deborah is a fascinating account, that in a few spots does not paint a complete picture. Like many parts of the Hebrew Bible, it is assumed we know enough to fill in some of the blanks on our own from things that all people knew thousands of years ago. Deborah is in her own way, an unlikely savior, as we are told she might be a bit bookish, and not the "rough rider" kind of judge that might have been talked about in previous tales. Yet, she has the quality of a superheroine.

Deborah begins, much like Wonder Woman in a way, as a judge in the ancient history of Israel, sitting beneath the tree in wisdom, aiding the people in seeing the best path to resolution and justice. Wonder Woman began on her island home of Themyscira, studying and training in the arts of the

Amazonian under many teachers and was valued by her mother the Queen of the Amazons as a wise counsellor.

Deborah hears a call, and gives it, as directed by God, to Barak. A message of war, and conquest. Wonder Woman, upon meeting Steve Trevor follows as a similar pull to the war effort of World War 2.

Deborah is the center of Barak's understanding of the power structure. "I won't go into war unless you are with me!" he says. And similarly, Wonder Woman takes the field of battle alongside Steve Trevor.

And when Deborah goes into the battlefield? Her story is a blockbuster account! It is a scene pulled from any summer movie. The special effects budget along would rival the battle scenes of "Saving Private Ryan" or "Lord of the Rings":

"When Sisera learned that Barak had led an army to Mount Tabor, he called his troops together and got all nine hundred iron chariots ready. Then he led his army away from Harosheth-Ha-Goiim to the Kishon River. *(Can you hear the trumpets calling as 900 pairs of horses come thundering along?)*

Deborah shouted, "Barak, it's time to attack Sisera! Because today the LORD is going to help you defeat him. In fact, the LORD has already gone on ahead to fight for you." *(Deborah has the wind in her hair as she pulls up running alongside him. She knows God is on their side and maybe even has a hint of a smile -- the confidence of God's prophet.)*

Barak led his ten thousand troops down from Mount Tabor. And during the battle, the LORD confused Sisera, his chariot drivers, and his whole army. Everyone was so afraid of Barak and his army, that even Sisera jumped down from his chariot and tried to escape. Barak's forces went after Sisera's chariots and army as far as Harosheth-Ha-Goiim. *(This is the big scene! Weapons are clashing, everything is chaos, the musical score is out of control and people are shouting as horses are squealing)*

Sisera's entire army was wiped out.

It's incredible! The movie would make millions! And in the lead of this epic story? This tale that would smash all the domestic records for the highest-grossing film? Deborah. At the head of the army, giving the order, shouting to Barak. There is a slow-motion scene in this movie: she raises her staff, shouting to Barak, hair flowing in the wind - "Now is the time!"

It's a very moving story.

We are told at the beginning of the account that this victory in battle is basically a reversal of an earlier allowance that God made for the country to be conquered. It was very normal for the people of Israel to see their conquest or freedom as a direct correlation to how close they were with God Almighty. When they were existing in freedom from oppression well that was when the people were close with God, experiencing who God is in daily life. When the conquerors came? It was because they had strayed from God's teachings.

The description of Jabin of Hazor's army is to drive home the point that Israel may very well never get out of this situation. Chariots, more so iron chariots, were the tanks, the M1A2 Abrams' tank of its day. It was like having 5,000 drones at your command. This many chariots gave this army an unstoppable fighting power. They were faster, stronger, and more deadly than anything else in existence at the time. For 20 years, they were the iron fist that enforced any whim the conquering king had. The people of Israel need someone to save them against this insurmountable enemy. They cry out for a hero.

Barak needs a hero as well. He comes off as a little unsure in these verses. Even though Deborah has told him of the Lord's command, he wants her to go with him. In fact, he's not going at all unless she goes! So Deborah steps away from the tree, and picks up her staff, and goes travelling with the army. And later in that crucial moment, she calls for the charge! She raises her hand!

Deborah the heroine.

Deborah is using what the Spirit of God has laid upon her to do in power because she loves her people. Because she loves the soldiers whose families she knows by name and heart. She has sat with them and their children as they came to her tree seeking wisdom. She does this because she is weary of the 20 years of suffering she has seen. Because she has heard from the Lord that the time has come to return to unity with God through the experience of freedom.

She follows what Paul is talking about in 2 Timothy, which I think is a pretty accurate description of what a hero or heroine really is. Don't be afraid, don't be a coward, Paul writes. That's not how God made you. God made you to have power, and love, and goodness in moderation[2]. Paul is reminding the young Timothy of Psalm 27;

"The Lord is my light and my salvation— whom shall I fear? The Lord is the stronghold of my life— of whom shall I be afraid?"

Go into this work unashamed. Unbowed. Act and speak for the Lord in that way that he created you. As a hero, as a heroine.

Deborah goes about her work as the wise woman beneath the tree in a time of great persecution. Twenty years worth. She is a well-known judge in this era, bringing hope against suffering (because how else would anyone be revered in a time of suffering?), and she is acting in that power of hope because of the love she had for God and the love she held for the suffering people around her. When the call came for action against the oppressors, she made new motions for the love of her people and shored up the will of Barak.

Like any good heroine, she inspired the troops. She lent her voice to the battle and brought that same fearlessness and unashamed attitude to

---

[2] [sōphronismos - used one time in the NT]

everyone who could hear her. She rallied them. She fired their hearts to do what God had in mind for them to do.

Like Wonder Woman at the vanguard of the battle.

Like Bree Newsome at the top of a flagpole. On June 27, 2015, Bree climbed up the controversial flagpole in Columbia, SC and took down the Confederate battle flag. She did this while the debate over the purpose and meaning of the flag continued on and in the wake of racist shootings and the vile burning of churches. I see what Bree did as the action of a heroine. She acts in the way Paul describes and in the way that Deborah acted. And in the way all our heroes and heroines act.

She was unafraid. She acted in love. She brought the power of hope.

Even as she began her climb up the pole the authorities demanded that she descend. Even though acting in such a way would make her a new target for hate groups. Even though she was climbing a flagpole that was three stories high. She was courageous. She was a heroine.

She perceived that the flag was causing harm, and injury, and pain to others. She perceived the deep harm and acted out of love for those suffering, for those who were vulnerable she acted, and in so doing brought the power of hope. As she took down the flag she recited Psalm 27 and prayed[3].

If you haven't followed the story she was arrested immediately after she climbed down and submitted herself to the local police.

For me, this story isn't about vandalism, but it is an inspirational tale about the incredible will and love that one woman had for others, and the fearless way in which she converted that love into action in the name of justice. Those are the actions of a heroine.

When we celebrate the Fourth of July, in essence, we are celebrating the notion that we have formed about what our country is. We form that picture, that image, that understanding, that emotion about our country largely from the stories of heroes and heroines. Alexander Graham Bell, Satchel Paige, Amelia Airheart, Nikola Tesla, Dorothea Lang, Ralph Bunche, Henry Ford, Maya Angelou, Katherine Graham -- countless others who make up our understanding of what our country is. Meaning not only the people in history who have worked to make this an amazing nation but the kinds of people we hope will continue to populate its history. Heroes and Heroines shape the way we see reality.

In ancient Israel, our friend Barrak knew this on some level. I can hear him saying, "Deborah! I need you! You have got to come with me into this battle. The men need you, their heroine, to inspire them as they face down hundreds of those iron death machines. Those weapons of war against which

---

[3] "Bree Newsome reflects on taking down South Carolina's Confederate flag 2 years ago" by Lottie Joiner, VOX Magazine

we have no hope - we need the power of the hope that you bring! I'm not going without you."

Our heroes and heroines shape our understanding of this country that we celebrate on the Fourth and the fabric of our lives, and so the implicit warning is here: beware of who you consider a hero and a heroine. Our readings from scripture this day take it one step further than that: beware of the kind of hero and heroine that you, yourself, become. Because that is what Paul and the story of Deborah are inviting us to become. Heroes and Heroines who in the power of hope that only God can bring we are asked to see people in love and speak for the Lord. Truly a task worthy of heroes and heroines.

And I want my daughter to be inspired as she lives and grows up. As she runs with her cape flapping in the wind I want her to know the stories of Biblical heroines like Deborah. And I want her to know the heroines of this more recent age as well when she seeks inspiration. Women like Malala Yousafzai who as a young girl stood against tyranny in her own country for the sake of equal education; Frida Khalo who brought incredible art out of a tortured life; Grace Hopper the mathematician who created the COBOL programming language; Audrey Hepburn, Temple Grandin, Ida May Gaskin and... Bree Newsome. I want her to hear the Godly hope and purpose that comes through these lives so that she too can live her life as a heroine in God's story of purpose of the Good News on this earth.

And so should we all be inspired to be those heroes and heroines to her and to each other and all people. Because Paul is inviting us to not be timid cowards, but to run, double fists out before us, and never balking at our advance but to briefly ask if our capes are flapping in the wind. God has placed his hands on us, and is sure of our faith and so asks us, "Act in power, act in love, and in the goodness of self-moderation. Bravely inspire, so that, like the story of Deborah and Barak, the people can come out of tyranny and into the freedom of a close relationship with Me."

When we act like heroes and heroines we have the power to change how people see God. We have the power to alter whether they fear the battle or go forward confidently into the fight ahead. We have the power, given by God, to show the world the kindness of God brought in Jesus Christ. We have the power to communicate the light that shines and offers a life that does not end. And that's a tall order, even for heroes and heroines, but God knows we can do it. Because of the heroes and heroines that have gone before. Because, as Paul says, of Timothy's mother Eunice, and grandmother Lois.

Because of the faith of our fathers and mothers that have gone before.

Because God has placed that same heroism and that same faith in each of us.

3
Injustice Anywhere

Written after the Manchester Arena was bombed in the United Kingdom

ECCLESIASTES 4
EPHESIANS 2:1-14

Whenever reading through the book of Ecclesiastes we are treated to the unique voice of the author whose name in Hebrew is "Qoheleth." So named after a feminine noun meaning something like "a voice that gathers folks together." In this reading, we hear about what Justice is like for the author, and in the usual style of the book, we have no relief in sight.

The Bible likes to talk about justice and the folks who preach or seek social justice in the world like to use scripture to defend or explain why they seek it. There are surely a lot of verses that deal with the idea and support our work for justice in the world, perhaps most notably the famous verse from Micah 6:8 remind that we are in fact required to "do justice" in a spirit of all humility. Isaiah describes God as a Lord of Justice[4], and even before Amos famously describes the good justice of God rolling down over all the earth[5], the Psalms remind us in several places that wickedness is doomed to perish[6] and the just, the truly righteous, are destined to prevail over all the earth. In the law of Deuteronomy and the wisdom of Proverbs the concept of good justice is repeated again and again. Christ himself makes a point to mention what justice looks like and the fact that God will see and bring justice for God's people in Luke 18 using the unjust judge as a parable. Justice is a major Biblical theme, and yet when we read the words of Qoheleth in the book of Ecclesiastes, I commiserate with the author, and wonder if you do too because it sounds like the world we experience, but not the world for which we may hope.

In the Contemporary English translation, verse 7 says, "Once again I saw that nothing on earth makes sense." Have you said this in the past week? The past year? Or in the past decade? We look at injustice in our city, or on the news across the country and the globe and there is a sense, a feeling that some part of what is happening is against the rule of the creator because it just doesn't make sense; when there is a bombing of a European arena or a drone attack that kills civilians; when there is a protest or a riot; when we

---

[4] Isaiah 61:8
[5] Amos 5:24
[6] Psalm 1:4-6, 125:3

witness underfunded schools or whole neighborhoods that commit to private education to steer clear of "urban" families; when we witness something unjust there is a sense in *us* that perks up and says "that doesn't make sense."

Our world is the world of Qoheleth. Chapter 4 describes a world that has people being mistreated *everywhere*. There is crying without comfort, and the dangers in this situation are powerful. Oppression is to the point in this world where the dead are better off than the living, but the ones who are even better off than the dead are the ones who have never been alive because they never had to experience what this world was like before the wealthy began destroying people's lives. That's bleak. Those are the words of a person who is witnessing the crisis of a generation that permeates every part of their existence.

The church is supposed to be very good about justice. The church is supposed to be God's hands and feet working toward justice on the earth, and maybe we all feel that impetus driving us forward into action. Maybe we see the incredible work that our church is doing to build partnerships with people who suffer under the rule of the powerful. And that is important work. When we do that work we align ourselves and put ourselves in touch with the authorship of scripture in a very tangible way. We cannot forget that the Bible was written from the voice of a people who were constantly being ruled over by one powerful Empire or another for thousands of years. The Assyrians, the Babylonians, the Romans... The majority of scripture is written from the voice of the oppressed and much of that was written either about people who were incarcerated by the justice system of the various empires or by the people who were themselves incarcerated as criminals. If we read it with a voice that does not feel systematic oppression and wrongful imprisonment then we are missing the story.

So doing justice work is important. We get that. And yet...

The author goes on to say that even when we do wonderful things we are only doing it because we are jealous of others. Well, darn. The rest of the Bible has the decency to at least imply that working at God's justice will at least get you a nod of well done good and faithful servant. But not Qoheleth. The author, in a wonderfully complex little simile poem, says that sure, some people do nothing (those who starve), but doing only very little is better than doing a lot that amounts to nothing.

Working, it seems, to have more, even to have more justice, is a futile endeavor. Some translations will say "chasing the wind" instead of meaningless. You can run after the wind, but you can't catch it, you will never arrive at the place that it started. Who cares if we work for justice? Who inherits our work after we are gone? Are they really going to be better off? Why should we work against something that seems to be as inevitable as injustice? The powerful, says Qoheleth, will always mistreat those without power. And even if they do something good, it's only because the powerful are jealous of each other and want to make a grand name for themselves.

At some point, I am supposed to share a story that will describe and solidify everything that I have been talking about. Which I could do. I have been reading this pretty incredible book called "Fist, Stick, Knife, Gun" by Geoffery Canada, which recounts his own experience with violence and injustice growing up in New York City. Yes, I could tell you a story from that book that highlights the seemingly inevitable route of injustice in the streets of America for millions of children growing up in the yesterday of the 1970's and the today of current culture, and I could also regale you with a story about my own life growing up in a small town on the banks of the Ohio River which did not, even in that place, escape the injustice of violence and the oppression of the powerful. Maybe that would draw lines of parallel for you to your own experience, or to what you have seen take place in the streets of Richmond. That the children who attacked me over my early school years for being different did so because their parents trained them that someone had to be oppressed in life for them to feel worthy, and that meant that kids like me who didn't fit in, or kids with different skin than them, were supposed to be deconstructed with violence. It's possible that would be meaningful to you and perhaps even spur you on to some kind of good action in the week, or weeks to come, and yet... That doesn't particularly sound like Good News to me. It sounds like Good-*ness*.

Good-*ness* is different from justice. It might sound like Good-ness would solve Qoheleth's little dilemma in the world that his words play witness to, but I think that Good-ness falls into the overwork that is really just wind chasing action that benefits no one in the long run.

We expect that Good-ness, a free-will action to choose moral paths will lead all people to succeed in our country. The idea of "free will" in this sense is a deadly trap, and I will say, wholly un-presbyterian. The goodness of an individual or the idea that subordinated groups can progress if they fit in and obey the rules of the establishment is a white-faced lie. If we really want to engage in God's sense of justice, then we will have to divest ourselves of decades and decades of teaching that says bad behavior is worse than inherent sinfulness. Isn't that how our thoughts sometimes lean? That the prostitute or the murderer's immoral action makes them lower in God's eyes than our own more minor sinfulness?

The early church knew the truth at their core, and Paul reminds them of it in this Ephesians reading. Early Christians were used to suffering for their beliefs. Their daily witness to who Jesus was greatly disturbed the people in the power structure of the day. That's what Good News does. Oppression comes from power. Good News came to do something different than to defend the establishment and preserve the status quo. In order for our actions to truly hold any meaning, we will have to do more than the simple wind-chasing of moralistic actions.

Alone we are doomed to wind chasing. Thankfully God has stepped in to change us.

Ephesians 2 is an incredible verse because "sin" can be read, and should be read, in many different ways. Sin is not what leads to death, sin is the *cause* of death. We, as sinful people are not on our way to death, we are in fact, dead. Only not currently dead. We *were* dead, Paul says. Paul does a great job as a writer to bait us with intrigue as he describes our death. What things lead to death? This is the wonderfully flexible part. "The ways of the world," says Paul. The ones who rule this world, that is the spirit of evil, and also desires that put ourselves first. The desires of our bodies and our minds. Misogyny, wealth, a disdain for our brothers and sisters in Christ, a focus on ourselves, a desire to do only things that please us, to talk about how great we are, the thought that the world should treat us well because of our station in life, seeking power, lying to protect ourselves or our positions -- all of these things are death and markers of a following of evil. And I am sure we could come up with more: Intellectual hubris (that's mine), racism, classism, fear of the other, or even fear itself belies our sinfulness is not trusting God as sovereign. I will let you fill in your own personal sins in this space rather than spend the day listing them.

But! In the Greek, there is this wonderful little word, *de*! Paul inserts it here as the fulcrum of what he has said and what he is going to say because it leverages our old life of death apart from our life found only in Jesus Christ. But, God is merciful. But, God loved us, sinful people, though we are, that we were raised from death to life with Jesus Christ. This is how we live differently.

We could moralize our way into something that seems like justice. We could work and strain and kill ourselves and not be actually doing anything but working from the idolatry of ourselves, creating ourselves as individual gods who are the center of values. We could use the church as a way to cultivate a therapeutic technique so that we may acquire meaning and joy in life.

But!

We could also bend away from that kind of narcissistic faith and instead lean towards God's gift to us. The bodily presence of Jesus Christ who loves us and saves us from death and who was sent to complete the work that God made us to do. To live, as a united people that have no walls of separation between us, and who act, not out of our own moral relativism because it's the right thing to do or the good thing that our friends and peers and social groups expect out of us, but who walk boldly out of the will of God witnessing to an amazing resurrection that was performed on us.

This is how we break Qoheleth's dire survey of the way we know the world to be. We can agree with Qoheleth and say, yes, the world of Injustice is rampant all around us, and it is better to be dead, and in fact, we have been dead. We know what death feels like,

But!

That wasn't the end of our story. We were raised in life.

Qoheleth's last word before going on to talk about worship is to recount a short parable about the new leader. Who came into power after the King was gone. This new ruler had followers that could not be counted, the new ruler is compared to a ruler who won't listen to advice...

But...

Years from now, no one will praise this ruler. The praise of this ruler is as meaningless as chasing after the wind -- so we as Christian disciples do not do such meaningless things. We have been raised to life by another power, a power which will still be in control of the universe in the years to come, and isn't something we obtained by anything we did. It was a gift. There can be no bragging, no power structure, no rulers and ruled in the kingdom of God because everyone was dead and brought to life through no actions that we performed. No merit of our own got us here. No color of our skin or wealth in our back account performed this action. No better or worse college degree, no vellum from esteemed institutions, no public or private school diploma. Only the amazing gift and grace of God. That is what inspires our way out of a life of death and clears our way to real Justice.

Qoheleth's view of justice is the view of moralism. The idea that human behavior is ever going to create real justice is just as ludicrous as the notion that this church or any church is the place where we good folk come to be or feel just a little bit more good. That's the lie of Good-ness verses Good News. The Good News is that this is a place built by sinful people, a place where sinful people who were once dead have been raised up again. Not that we are now wholly without sin every day, but that we can get up each day, open our eyes and bear witness to the Grace of Jesus Christ which persistently and pervasively creates new life in us.

Upon waking we look out across the unjust world and say, "Yes, once again I see that nothing on earth makes sense."

But!

Though I am not full of good-ness, I am full of Good News. With Christ, the fight for justice through the Gospel is possible, and not just chasing the wind. We have been raised *new* this morning, and we are made to witness to that resurrection and to the power and care of real Justice.

4
It's Woe for Everyone

Written as people fled death in Syria and sought new homes in the world

ECCLESIASTES 3:9-21
MATTHEW 11:20-30
ISAIAH 22:17-24

Everything is worthless and empty.
    That's the takeaway from this reading. At least, it is through the lens of our world. Isn't that how it feels? Isn't that what we are even, perhaps, afraid to say?
    Ecclesiastes is sometimes a hard book of the Bible to read. It's a little esoteric. It's a little jaded and ends with bleak conclusions that "no one can find the best ways of acting and no one can know the future." It ends the way it begins, with the famous lines: "Vanity of Vanities, all is vanity." Which in the original Hebrew translates to be something more like emptiness, or absurdity or a vacuum of meaninglessness. It's a strange book. No wonder we don't read it more often.
    Its author, for whom the book is named, in Hebrew has the title *Qoheleth*. The name Ecclesiastes is the Greek attempt at the Hebrew. The Hebrew itself is a little oddly ambiguous, sharing possible roots with the verb for "assembling" and "speak." Our best answer right now is that it was some kind of moniker given to the assembler of the wisdom, or to a speaker, or preacher, or just simply -- The Gatherer.
    This verse from chapter 3 is a well-known one by many of us; it's where the idea of "eat, drink and be merry" has its origin. Something that scripture itself echoes in Luke 12:19, and in Isaiah 23:13. It is not, however, proposing a hedonistic lifestyle. It's not putting forward the Biblical backing for a life of selfishness. It is accepting the loss of control that humans have in comparison to the authority of God. The last part of verse 13 of this reading says clearly; that life is God's gift, and that our merriment comes in our toil, that is, our "work." The things we do, our calling, our actions. Our lives.
    Ultimately, the work of the universe is God's work, and as we have a Just God, we can trust that the work will be done justly. In that same vein, Qoheleth, the Gatherer, speaks. Our human selfishness or human jadedness reads into this wisdom book and places things here that aren't intended.
    All the talk of dust and death, and questions about where the human spirit goes afterwards can be a little disheartening, but the main purpose of

the entire book is that human understanding cannot compare to God and that our lives are tied to the other creatures that God has made. We all live, eat, breathe, and die, on the same planet. Our control is an illusion that we have created. Qoheleth's words do not shy away from the very hard idea that you can't take it with you. And also reflects that the mystery of life should be enjoyed as we are gifted the time we have to enjoy it.

And really, the Gospel of Matthew has Jesus saying the same thing.

Doesn't it? Perhaps, what we might call, a litany of woe, doesn't sound like an invitation to enjoy life.

We are met in this verse from Matthew with a warning. A warning in which Jesus is following a model created by the prophets of old. Prophets that everyone would have been familiar with, and this style would have piqued their interest, it would have tipped them off to re-remember those prior verses. Verses like Jerimiah 2-11, Ezekiel 24, Amos 2:4-3:8, and Micah 1:9-15. But more interestingly, Jesus is almost quoting directly from Isaiah 22. The warning of the destruction of Jerusalem. In this chapter of Isaiah the prophet warns:

> Your rulers have all fled together;
>   they were captured without the use of a bow.
> All of you who were found were captured,
>   though they had fled far away.
> Therefore I said:
> Look away from me,
>   let me weep bitter tears;
> do not try to comfort me
>   for the destruction of my beloved people.

This is all standard destruction of the city kind of stuff. Bitter tears, a lot of weeping, but where it really gets interesting is a little bit further down:

> In that day the Lord GOD of hosts
>   called to weeping and mourning,
>   to baldness and putting on sackcloth;
> but instead, there was joy and festivity,
>   killing oxen and slaughtering sheep,
>   eating meat and drinking wine.
> "Let us eat and drink,
>   for tomorrow we die."

First of all, we have a call to repentance, specifically to sackcloth, which Jesus has mentioned. But also, there is an understanding that the people were not repenting and were instead doing what? Eating and drinking... For tomorrow we die.

In a very "Inception" kind of moment, Jesus is referring to a passage from Isaiah that itself is referring to passages from Ecclesiastes. And there is a reason for that. Jesus does this on purpose.

Further in this passage from Isaiah, the prophet gets to the meat of what he is talking about: the denunciation of self-seeking officials. And the language is serious:

" The Lord is about to hurl you away violently, my fellow. He will seize firm hold on you, whirl you round and round, and throw you like a ball into a wide land; there you shall die, and there your splendid chariots shall lie, O you disgrace to your master's house! I will thrust you from your office, and you will be pulled down from your post."

Incidentally, This is the first recorded baseball reference in history.

This is where Jesus is coming from. This is the deeper message behind his words and it is absolutely intentional, and the people who heard it in the first century absolutely heard it that way.

This wasn't a random call to the cities. This was a specific, targeted, message. To the officials. To the rich. To the ones who thought they were the chosen people of God. Jesus is calling them out. Later in verse 29, Jesus says that he has a gentle and humble heart. That is to be taken in stark contrast to the people he is talking about in the earlier verses. Those who refuse to repent. Those who are falsely humble and not gentle of heart.

We are met with the same warning. "Be careful or there is an eternity of woe just around the corner." It's not a soft message. Sodom will have had it better than us. A city and a people who were destroyed by fire and sulfur being rained down on them from the sky so that every creature and every plant died in agony got off easy by comparison. The land is described as the smoke that goes up from a furnace. Waves of heat coming off of it. A choking gas released from the ground. That's the woe of the unrepentant. The self-serving. Those who cannot be gentle. Or humble.

We are like the prosperous cities of Judea. Of Capernaum and all the rest. Our privilege cripples us. It starts us at a moral loss. We are already in the negative. It is so much easier for us to misinterpret the words of Qoheleth. To think that we have had something to do with our incredible station in life. It is to the point now that doing nothing is not enough. You see, that is the point at which the cities around Galilee were. They weren't actively harming anyone. They weren't persecuting anyone. They were leading simple lives. Good lives. Lives that maybe followed most of the commandments of Jewish law, sure. They stayed out of politics perhaps. Let other lands fend for themselves. They agreed to disagree and kept the peace. But it's not enough. Being stationary isn't enough, simply believing the right thing, accepting the Grace of Christ isn't enough. Just witnessing the miracle isn't enough.

So, what does Jesus want with us?

Those among us who think we have it all figured out. Who think we can tell each other that the Godly life should look like this, or repentance should look like that; Jesus says that the truth has been hidden from the wise, and given to infants. "You don't know what you think you know," says Jesus. This is a joke, by the way, an interjection that Jesus uses, a little humor to make what he is going to say stick. If you watch, Jesus is often very funny before he hits people with something really profound. Because then he says this: "I have God's full authority." Do you want to know God? Then look at what Jesus has been doing. Jesus says, "Know me, and know the father."

He's been talking about all the miracles. He's saying at this point, "You should know who I am, and who I am is who God *is*. This is the 11th chapter. By this point in Matthew, we know who Jesus is too: The son of God who came with a message so life-changing that families would be torn apart by it. A power that nothing else in heaven or earth can withstand. A forgiver of sins. A lover of the unloved. A healer of the faithful, who made no distinction between God's children. A hater of hypocrites, and of those people who fool themselves and others into thinking they are faithful. A teacher who expected and demanded real action from his students. A prayerful rabbi who sought humility, faithful giving, and a lack of worry in this life above other earthly treasures. A savior who cried out in the world for a Love of enemies, and preacher of social and political justice who was about liberation. The Christ. The beloved. We know who Jesus *is*, and so we know what God is like.

We know. And it's only chapter 11.

What does Jesus want from us? That we know him. That we know God.

That we realize our active participation is needed and demanded and encouraged and written into the code of our DNA and the fabric of our spirits.

And when we do this, when we are active, we should enjoy it.

We should revel in it.

We should be merry just like Qoheleth implores us because everything is God's.

Yet, we tell ourselves and each other that the work of God is tiring.

We say to ourselves that we are tired of fighting for what we think is right, or for God's *real* Kingdom and that is the crux of our problem. Fighting for God's purposes is fighting upstream truly, and can legitimately be tiring. It often is making a way out of no way.

I thought the burden is supposed to be easy and the yoke light, yet we are worn out and spiritually tired and unsatisfied. Something is amiss.

It's not about what we think is right. It's not about our little feeling of uneasiness. Or comfort. Qoheleth echoes in our brains. Vanity. *Vanity.* And

Jesus responds, "how dare you." How dare you witness the miracles I have set before you and not repent. Woe to you. Woe to you.

We should celebrate the light yoke in the midst of our struggle. There are scores of people who fight for justice every day who keep these similar key things in mind. Leah Lewis, a film-maker and writer who has been featured in IOBY's Racial Justice Toolkit, reminds all of us that it is important in the upstream arc of our lives to find our own sense of restoration, remember the good being done, and to allow ourselves patience in the work. Rome wasn't dismantled in a day, after all. So then, we can and should celebrate and recognize the miracles of our own church family. Simple things like people teaching Sunday school from week to week. Those helping out a refugee family in desperate need in a new country. Folks that have been devoting years of their lives to the service of the church. Visiting with those who are sick and lonely. Those who pray every week for one another. On and on and on our lists of miracles could go for hours every week. Seeing this in each other, bearing witness to the miracles isn't hubris. It's a testimony. That's the joy in the work we do. That's the lightness of the yoke and the ease of the burden.

Physically these things can be draining if we don't allow for our own care.

But spiritually, we should walk out of this building every week nourished and fed and bright-eyed and amazed at what God has done in our midst. What God has done in the midst of our community and our city and our world.

Augustine says this in one of his sermons:

"Lo, how sweet a yoke of Christ did he bear, and how light a burden; so that he could say that all those hard and grievous sufferings at the recital of which as just above every hearer shudders, were a "light tribulation;" as he beheld with the inward eyes, the eyes of faith,"

He uses this example too:

"To what storms and tempests, to what a fearful and tremendous raging of sky and sea, do the busy merchantmen expose themselves, that they may acquire riches inconstant as the wind, and full of perils and tempests, greater even than those by which they were acquired!"[7]

We do crazy things for work that we love.

We have an alternative to a life of misery, to a life of woe, and in fact, those who cannot claim the yoke of Christ are doomed to woe as well. Do we know people who have a beautiful home, a loving family, all the food they could want, a decent job, and all the rest -- but are still miserable? These folks who are endlessly searching or malcontent with the amazing blessing of life

---

[7] St. Augustine: Sermon on the Mount; Harmony of the Gospels; Homilies on the Gospels, Sermon XX

that sits with them every day. Who endlessly chases promotion or more wealth or notoriety? Are *we* those people? Do we dare to tempt the prophecy Christ makes by living in the midst of the miracle and never ever realizing it? Are we in the grip of blessing, but refuse to take our proper joy in it? Are we in the grip of stability, but refuse to seek the real welfare of others because of what it might "cost us?"

Qoheleth and Augustine are saying much the same thing: "Life, as God has made it, is for our Joy." If we do not actively work into that we are doomed to a world of woe. God has little patience for entitled fragile people.

Remember that as Jesus is speaking in this Matthew passage, he mentions Tyre and Sidon which were in Syria. These were not the chosen people of God. We know that Jesus is constantly telling the people of Israel, "This message is going out worldwide. You don't have the corner market on being God's people anymore." It's the same message to us, right here in our churches.

We have never had the corner market. If we do not see the miracle of life that is around us, the opportunity for justice, or the deep need for loving evangelism in our city... then woe to us. There are others outside these doors who will.

This life in Christ, this faith, this being a Christian thing is an active thing. It is not a passive work. It is a daily practice and an hourly discipline. It's a movement, not a moment. It is a ministry filled minute to minute with engaging words. It is not enough to just be the city in which the miracles happen, like Capernaum. We cannot just be "Christ adjacent."

We are to be as Christ. To *repent*, and take on the mantle.

We are to be the embodied challenge to a world filled with disgusting hatred for one another. To fly in the face of every part of anyone who would deny a brother or sister their rightful place in a world that we did not create. In a world that we are merely supposed to oversee. And as Qoheleth reminds us, we are made of the same stuff as the animal kingdom. We are all in this together. We are all going to suffer and succeed in the same air, and drinking the same water.

So then, if there are brothers and sisters who are being killed unfairly in the streets? And we say nothing? Woe to us. If there are God's human creations who are imprisoned at a glaringly unfair ratio? Then woe to our sense of justice. If there are people who starve for nutrition as they desperately eat cheap food that creates obesity and diabetic blindness in children? Then woe to us. If there are people who weep as they flee conflict, poverty, and plague, and we do nothing? Or worse yet block their flight to safety? Then woe to us. If there is hatred in the hearts of our city, no matter how well disguised, and we refuse to see it or speak out against it? Then woe to us. The kind of woe that would make the destruction of Sodom look like a summer holiday.

This is the message of Jesus Christ as he stands and looks at the cities that have witnessed countless miracles! He rails at them and says the people of the pagan gods would repent and witness to who is God faster than you bunch of unbelievers.

This is serious. These are Jesus' words. He then re-enforces it by saying, "hey folks, this is who I am. This is who *God* is. This is the deal." Do you see deeds of power without getting on board the Jesus train? It's not going to go well for you.

"Come to me," Jesus says.

"If you don't know what the blessings of life are, if you are afraid you are surrounded by the miracles and can't see them, if you don't want to be part of the condemnation of woe... Then come to me. Because the life I have for you is light. The work that we do together is easy." Because, as Augustine points out -- it is joyful work.

The idea that we should lament our losses and wring our hands in fear of the future is not scriptural. It's not Christ like, and if we are to take what Christ is saying seriously, it's not the way of a faithful person. It is that way of Woe. The idea that we think we can keep separate our church life and our secular life is a lie. That our understanding of love in Christ shouldn't inform our political opinion is not faithful. It's not the way of Christ expecting action from his disciples.

So we can give up on the way of woe. We are called to stop trying to explain away our narrow position on who gets to have love, and justice, and joy. Qoheleth tells us, those things aren't ours anyway. They are bigger than us.

We are meant for Joy, in realizing that God is the center of all. We don't need to be trapped in anger and fear and distrust and worry and hate and disgust. We don't have to live in a condemned city, destroyed in fire and wallowing in pain.

We are invited. To take a rest. To find the humble and gentle heart of Christ. To take an easy yoke and a light burden. To find joy in our work together.

Because the way of woe is death. The way of Christ is our only path to real life.

5
The Cost of Unity

Written during Black History Month in Richmond, VA

PSALM 133
EPHESIANS 4

The Dismantling Racism ministry group that I am a part of recently finished our Bible study curriculum that was made available to churches in our Presbytery. It's a collaborative work that we've been putting together over the past few months, as a way for churches to begin the work of *engaging* with racism, and as the name of our purpose groups suggests, commit to *dismantling* the racism that is present in our world.

The group has been a blessing to me personally, as it has given me the excuse to pair with some really amazing people this past year during our efforts in building the curriculum. We held a retreat to help that work in January of this year, and we just sat and talked together about how to even make the space available to our own churches so they could begin or enrich their education along this good path. What we most desired was for a large group of people, from many backgrounds, all along a spectrum of understanding, to share bravely what it was that they or their church believed. Earlier this year at a lunch we hosted for our churches, educators and ministry leaders we had just that. Much like the experiences I have had in Richmond's "Coming to the Table" group, it seemed good just to be in that space where voices about where our churches were could be shared openly. The purpose of it was not to condemn one another or solve any issue, but to hear each other, and through that -- to listen for what the Spirit had to say to the church. Which is no easy thing.

We heard a lot of comments afterward that were deeply appreciative of that time we made to talk. Or rather, not just to talk together and to hear the voices of others from whom they did not normally hear, but to also know that they were not alone in the work of finding or being on the path.

It made me realize; we spend a lot of time alone.

There is a book called "Them: Why we hate each other -- and how to heal," by Ben Sasse, that uses large sections to address the idea of being alone. In the book, it notes the heatwave of 1995 in Chicago and the 739 people that died in that week because of the heat. So many people ran their AC units to beat the 120-degree heat index, that the city's power grid shut off. Without access to cool air, hundreds died, and it was such a divergence from their normal mortality rate that morgues had to rent refrigeration trucks to store the bodies. It took a sociologist, Eric Klineburg, five years to nail down why the death tolls seemed to align themselves along neighborhood lines. That is, some neighborhoods fared better and some worse in terms of how many people died there. Through his study, he found that those neighbors who knew who was old and sick and alone would check in on them. In neighborhoods that were abandoned by service providers, and hosted solitary residents, the deaths were exponentially higher. In the neighborhoods of solitary people, in those places where an interwoven community did not reside, it took weeks to find the bodies of people that had passed. Weeks.

Psalm 133 says, "How good and pleasant it is, to dwell together in unity..." When we are alone we die. We suffer. Isolation turns something that is dangerous into something can be deadly. We can isolate alone, or even in a small pod, but the result is much the same. Suffering and fear.

We know that isolation isn't good for us, but there are all kinds of isolations that we experience nonetheless. In the whole letter of Ephesians, Paul is inflamed by the Spirit to write out why and how the breaking of the church into tribes, or isolated communities within the church, are inherently against the Gospel that Jesus came to bring. That further, even if they were unified as a church, any further segregation from the rest of the community would still be against the purpose of a real disciple of Christ. In the very first verse of chapter 4, some translations will say "live a life," others will say "walk," which I like better because it is closer to the Greek words here. Because the intention of the Greek word is the kind of "walk" that you take in order to live. The walk that carries you through every part of your life. To the grocery, the school, the workplace, the home -- essentially, "Everywhere that your feet take you." That is where Paul is begging the church to go and "be" in the way intended for them by God. As a community, as a fellowship, further described in the following verses, he again reminds the church, "You are One." One calling which brings us, one Lord, one faith and baptism within our faith, and further, One God of all of Creation.

The Holy Spirit inspires Paul to write this to the church of several thousand years ago, and it inspires us to listen to it today. It is no more or less true for all that intermittent time. It matches for Paul, the Hebrew understanding of the *goodness* of unity. The Psalmist's "How good it is..." to be cared for by a neighbor. How pleasant to be one in unity together. It's an inherent good. It is the life that God intends from the first moments of creation as we know, two were created when one just wouldn't suffice. It is the life that God means for us to have at the end of all things when we read about the Holy City in Revelation whose gates are never shut, and which practices the radical openness of God meant for the whole of the world. Anything that creates disunity is sin, and the wages of sin, as we know, are death.

I was amazed to find that as I read Ben Sasse's book what are the biggest killers in 2016, outside of Heart Disease and Cancer? Does anyone want to guess? Write it out on a slip of paper? It's three things: Alzheimer's, suicides, and unintentional injuries -- that last one makes the list because it includes drug overdose. Drug overdoses are almost twice the number of car accidents per year, which long held the title as our biggest killer. In 2019, the numbers of these three types of death have gone up, and though they lost their top spot they still feature in the top ten. In 2016, the number of suicides hit a 30 year high, a trend which has continued. The author's point of these harrowing statistics is that we are dying, most of all, from despair. The isolation we feel, which we sometimes purposefully and sometimes incidentally reinforce, is killing us on a national level.

"How good and pleasant it is to dwell together in unity…"

Some folks who don't think that the church is the proper place to talk about racism. Perhaps that comes out of the knowledge of how scripture was perverted and twisted for so many years to support the sin of chattel slavery and Jim Crow racism, in this very city, perhaps from this very pulpit. Certainly, in any church that is older than the Civil War, the gospel was twisted to meet the demand of society. Our reluctance to talk about racism in the church now perhaps stems from a fear of the Gospel being too harsh on a place that forgot what unity actually looked like for so long. It must bear a place in our meditation on these verses as we read them 400 years past those most dark and perverse days. Are afraid of the word "racism?" Afraid that it has such a large load of baggage we cannot bear it, or approach it? It is important for us to talk about. As the church. As Christians. As people who are on this "walk" in our lives. As people whose "walk" takes them along this street of monuments, and in this capital which was once the place of slave pens and auction blocks. As a people whose "walk" takes us to all the places that our feet carry us in our lives are in desperate need of the unity of Christ that we were meant to experience. We are in need of this imperative of the Gospel, and of this revelation of God's intention for the world.

So we must talk about it.

No matter what our fear or trepidation. Through those emotions we must trust God's spirit as it reaches across the differences of background and education. We are built as the body of Christ, which creates new connective tissue across cultural distinctions and all the contrasting kinds of traumas we've experienced. This isn't a smoothing over of our edges into a homogenous soup of Christianity. This is an individually gifted, many parted body -- the multi faceted faithful kind of unity. One Faith, one baptism, one Lord, One Bread, One Body, One cup of blessing, and within that, all of the beautifully diverse pieces of the whole bearing one another in love.

"How good and pleasant it is…"

Coming to the Table, which I mentioned before, is based on a Quaker model of coming together. The intent is to bring people across the spectrum and experience of race into the same room and to have them talk, make mistakes, and eat with one another. There are some guidelines to keep things loving, and there is usually a facilitator, but the purpose is not to solve or fix anything or anyone, but to share and listen and hear. There was a phrase that I heard a lot while I was there in those meetings, and in some of our presbytery conversations; "I never knew." Someone would share their experience or their hurt or their intention, and people of every color, with a sense of kindness and understanding, would say the same thing; "I never knew."

We are alone, it seems.

Racism is one of the opposing forces that run counter to God's will of unity and wholeness for the world. If we don't keep talking about it, hearing experiences, sharing our hurt, exposing our ignorance, then we will *only* live in the world of "I never knew." We will only live in a world alone, without the Unity that God has in mind for us.

When we speak the truth in love, Paul says, we grow into our true maturity as Christians. When we hear one another. When we listen. That is when we become the *real* church with Christ at our Head. "I never knew," is the door chime of maturity coming to visit. For Paul, what is the alternative to speaking our truth to one another in love? Darkness and non-understanding. Separated living. Impurity and greed. From her book "Dust Tracks On the Road," african-american anthropologist and author Zora Neale Hurston said, "there is no agony like bearing an untold story inside of you." It seems Paul would agree. Speaking to one another, telling our stories of truth and most importantly, truly hearing them in love, *or* living in agony and isolation. That is what is at stake.

Living into our roles as people who are committed to dismantling the racism that can separate us, sets us on the path of unity that has so long been divided by our social institutions. The church still suffers from self-inflicted wounds that broke communities into pieces and systematically established the walls and chasms that separate our communities in this city ideologically and physically. In the midst of this reality, Paul brings us hope. The psalmist reminds us of how good it can be. The blessing of unity has been commanded by God, and it is like cool dew on a hot and dry mountain. It is like a soothing oil on places in our bodies that have been worn and withered from the sun and our labor. It is so good and pleasant.

It is what the church is meant to be when it grows up.

It is how we live every part of our lives.

It is the fullness of what we were created, and gifted, and called to be.

God is proud of a church full of folks who are on that path, walking in their lives, already answering part of the fullness of the call. We know that we have been on the path, not finished with the work, but on the path, with one another within the church as we reach out to each other and have more conversations that require our courage, and as we continue to love and care for one another, to know one another, to check in on one another, to speak our truth in love to one another. How do we use the blessing of our endowment funds to aid our local communities and to overturn the narrative of hate? How do we continue to deepen our relationship with those who challenge us? How do we continue to build our community out in a widening circle to the city still healing from decades of injustice, and on into the world.

We will continue to confront racism and division wherever they lie because they are *against* God and the hard work of unity that God means for the church to dwell within. I know we will continue on this path no matter the cost to us, our pride or our accounts because it is, as we know, so good and so pleasant to do so.

6
Not Just my Feet

Written after the anniversary of the 2013 Boston Marathon Bombing

JOHN 13:1-17
EXODUS 12:1-14
GALATIANS 5:22-24

In all the times I have heard or read this passage the voice of Simon Peter changes slightly and my impression of him does as well. At my first reading, it sounded like simple overzealousness. "No, no Lord, I know who you are, I know who sent you, you aren't going to wash my feet." Then Jesus' words came back at him, and he replied "Well then if that is the case then don't stop at my feet! Wash all of me! I want to have as much a share with you as possible! Scrub me down every inch!" (I have a Baptist friend who jokes with me about our differences in baptism practices and I tell him, you know, all the apostles needed was to get their feet wet.)

To be honest, the more I get to know Simon Peter the less I like him. On my second and third readings of the passage I imagine this scene, which seems to imply that Simon Peter was not the first in line for this ceremony. That it was only when Jesus *came* to Simon Peter that he said something. Makes me think that the whole time James and John and the others are being bathed he's just waiting for his chance. Is it possible he is rubbing their noses in it a little?

"Oh no, Jesus. *I* get it. I have been paying attention. I am going to pass this little test that the others have failed as they sit quietly." Cue his satisfied smirk.

Is Simon Peter really being that competitive? His second statement sounds like backpedalling to me, an attempt to stay ahead of the pack after Jesus' admonishment. Jesus's reply is "No, this is enough." What I have given you is enough. This is *enough* to change you forever, this is enough to change the *world*. If you can do as I do in this mode of love that serves without competition, without hubris, then you can be called a blessing and be blessed.

I, of course, don't like Simon Peter because I don't like that I can act just like him. Turning a beautiful message about servanthood and the love and care we show each other because of the Grace of God into a competition. A measuring stick that becomes more about who *I* am instead of who God is. During this season of Lent we have been working through the fruits of the spirit. In that verse from Galatians, Paul admonishes the reader against conceit, and hubris -- exactly what I think Simon is showing here because of the same reason Paul is cautioning against it. It's not about you man. It's not about how great you are, or how much you know, or how well you preach, or if you "get it" ahead of the class. It's about how well you are communicating who God *is* to everyone around you.

In order to do that well you have to have a great deal of trust.

Without that you have a problem like Simon-Peter has. A problem that says "I am important, just as important, as the call God has on my life." My security, my comfort, my notions of success, my message, my ministry -- when these thoughts take precedence over our emulating the servanthood of Christ, we are like Simon Peter trying to save face, thinking we do the right thing for the right reason because we are unable to deal with the fear of loss that accompanies full trust.

Full trust *is* a loss.

We might not think about it in those terms, but it is a loss of our own power to control the world around us. We are attached to our notions. Our sense of self. The construct that we make. Our bodies, our image, our thoughts they become *who* we are. The servant created by God, who we truly are, gets lost in all that.

This construct of self is why I think our feet are hard to look at sometimes. We can call them ugly, or gross, or old. They can remind us of our mortality, our frailty, and our abject humanity as they tie us to the ground day after day. They hurt, wear out, and betray us causing us to stumble. They are usually hidden and so to reveal them is to uncover a kind of truth about ourselves. One that might disagree with the constructed self that we have made. We think ourselves demure and delicate, or strong and capable eternally -- one look at our feet might tell a different story. It takes a lot of trust to show someone our feet.

Passover and Easter this year coincide with the anniversary of the Boston Marathon bombing. With reflections of that event being in the news it got me thinking about how the marathon is a thing practically built around the foot. Runners everywhere! Brightly colored shoes! Pads, ointments and salves at every corner being sold and advertised by hundreds of booths. Every runner is intimately acquainted with their feet. They know where every blister and hot spot is about to occur, they have different ways to tie the right and left shoe for maximum effectiveness. They soak and baby their feet to honor them as they are perhaps the most important part of this machine called the runner. It is the place, after all, where the rubber literally meets the road.

Heather Abbot[8] was one of the victims of the bombing last year. She was lucky enough not to lose her life, but wears a prosthetic foot these days

---

[8] Women's Health magazine article, "It's been a trying year—but Heather is ready to return to the finish line." by Robin Hilmantel

complete with 4-inch heels. Heather has a total of 6 different feet now, in fact. A list that includes a waterproof model, her own design that is made for heels, and a running blade. She plans on running the marathon again.

Heather wasn't a runner before, however after losing her leg in the explosion has run a lot for charities supporting survivors.

In an interview with NPR[9], she said that it took her a while to really resonate with what was her new normal. In the midst of that, she has been counselling other amputees, especially women, about finding a positive outcome in loss.

Heather had to decide whether or not to allow doctors to amputate her foot. That was a choice, Abbott says, that was not really much of a choice at all.

"The life that was described to me, with keeping my leg, was not one I wanted," she explains. "I would be in chronic pain, and I was going to be pretty much wheelchair-bound."

Still, the decision kept her up at night in tears. That she had to make that choice herself rather than just waking up to find it done to her did give her a small sense of control at a time when she felt anything but.

Though even now in her positive and more healed mindset she has fear about how she will cope once the national and personal attention about the event disappears. In her own words, she says she worries it will get hard for her when people don't care anymore.

We talk about losing our lives as Christians, but what we really mean is a total loss of the life we used to have or a complete change of perception and understanding that forever alters us. In effect, giving us that new normal in a drastic way. That level of trust, that level of change, can feel very much like loss, with all the pain and grief and anger that comes with it, and I find we don't think about that very often. We assume that joy is the only allowable emotion in giving our lives to Christ, but people who experience loss I think are more like Heather -- who was incredibly joyful that she still had her life, but still struggled through all of those other loss emotions as well.

Full trust, complete trust *is loss*.

It is the exposure of our feet without the construct of our own self.

It is a full acceptance of what is *enough*.

Our best work in this "new life" is in counselling other amputees, or people who are afraid to lose their lives -- who are afraid of diving into that complete trust. That relationship with those who struggle -- we call that spreading the message of the Gospel. Like Heather, we are all on a circuit of speaking engagements even though we might not have an agent setting them all up ahead of time.

---

[9] //tinyurl.com/heather4inchheels

As we do this work in discipleship we begin to see the positive outcome in loss. Our mourning for the losses of self and our own expectations or demands begin to subside, and we start getting accustomed to our new normal and realizing the better completeness that accompanies that trust.

Our feet are different because of something earth shattering that happened long ago.

And like Heather, we sometimes fall back into fear, because we realize how much we depend on the care of the people around us. We depend on it in no less real a way that Heather does her support network.

Simon Peter wasn't ready for that loss at that moment. He needed to regain control of a situation that made him feel uncomfortable. "These other apostles might be ok with letting the master wash their feet but not me. I need to keep my constructed self. I can't yet give that up. I am going to say something." He attempts to wrangle authority of how this scene was going to play out because he just isn't ready to give into that complete trust.

He is telling Jesus, "I don't think you understand. People are looking up to me... There are bills to pay... My kids need braces... That move would take us too far away... This isn't what I have been working for my whole life... She is going to throw her life away if I don't intervene... That grade is going to make me or break me... I can't walk without my leg..."

He can't bear for Jesus to see his feet, to see his life completely laid bare.

He's trying to control the "enough" of his life, instead of hearing that he is enough.

We see Jesus clad as scripture describes him with the basin and the cloth. Dirty, wicked feet are going in. Dust and sand stuck between the toes, scrapes and calluses, bruises and pains washed and massaged away. Then they are removed from the water, and wiped with care. The soaked skin is softer, the dirt removed, and the towel rubs out the last of the aches.

Simon Peter sees this and something in him is thinking, "I can't walk on those feet."

This little trust is in a way a preparation for the days of silence in the tomb that are to come. Jesus is constantly coaxing all of us, trust a little more, trust a little more. Jesus gets to Peter and says as he tries to take his foot, "Simon Peter let me have control of this situation so that you are ready for the resurrection."

The Simon and Simones of this world, we the people who are afraid of the new normal that comes with new feet, we are invited into this place of trust. The Passover rituals were a striking lesson in trust and the fierce repercussions that lack of trust in the Word of God could have. Jesus's actions of servanthood are surely an invitation to serve one another, but more deeply in that story is a powerful invitation to trust. The two are linked. God knows that we human creatures cannot serve if we are not steeped in complete trust. The true servant is the one who can trust with total abandon.

This day is a remembrance for us. The powerful son of God who washed our feet and invited us to do the same. Jesus Christ, who showed us what real trust in the Will of God looks like through his passion, and told us that we should do the same.

Real trust requires sacrifice, it requires loss, it requires the revelation of our whole selves. It can only be done if we have the courage to face the loss of who we think we are and are willing to move forward in trust. If we can release our need to control this situation and let the master wash our feet, no matter what we look like, then we are truly prepared to be blessed people of the resurrection serving in love, at full peace, and ready to run again.

7
It's the Un-withered Leaf

Written in the heat of record summers in Virginia and the east-coast

PSALM 1
ROMANS 8:22-30

My wife's family has a long history in this country. So, naturally I, having a deep historical bug in my bones, was actually delighted to find that they already had a book dating the family line on her father's side back to 1609, where the family's destiny started in Lapersville, a small community in what is now Switzerland as Jorg Dallenbach made the choice to emigrate from his home.

I was, in fact, more interested in this than Leah or any of her siblings.

We came across the book while visiting her grandmother in upstate New York at the family farmhouse. The rest of the family had known about the book for years, but it was a treasure to me. My family, or the Lebanese half anyway, would just shrug when I asked them anything about the "old country" or the family history or stories from the distant past. Even though it had barely been a single generation since they came to America, I was usually told some variation on "Who knows what happened. There were fires; records were burned up. What are you so worried about?" Trying to explain the difference between wonder and worry to my great aunts was pretty useless.

At Leah's grandmother's farm, I spent the next few days reading and copying notes from the book, and every once in a while popping out my head and saying very interesting things like, "did you know your name used to be Dallenbach?" and "the guy is from Switzerland? His first name was Jorg. Isn't that cool?" Every time I said something I was met with varying degrees of, "Yeah," and some head nodding. I had the distinct impression I was being humored, but I didn't care. I forged on using the book to track down Leah's father's specific string of male heirs through time and space. A few came inland from the coast seeking jobs as tar-men, those who spent their days making coal tar from the mines, and were joined by other German speakers in a wave of immigration in the later 1700s. These folks were from the Palatine province of the Rhine River, and gave the name to the nearest town to Leah's grandmother's farm: Palatine Bridge, New York! See? It is very interesting, isn't it?

In all this reading, at one point, her Dad said something like, "Yeah I think there are some old graves out in the cow pasture south of the house." Which had me out of the door before he could punctuate the sentence. Upon investigation, this was a family plot that went back to the late 1700's and it held the grave of a very interesting Dillenback and his 2 wives. The graves themselves had been lost in the canopy of a surrounding grove of lilacs.

Leah and I stood out there talking, and I learned that their last name actually meant, "Tree by the river." I tried to trace back the original actual etymology of the name, but the closest I could get was the German for "Regal Bath" - Gallen Bad - which might have some merit. But they had a painted family crest of a tree sitting by a river in the annals of her grandmother's attic, so who was I to argue with family lore?

I think of Leah's family every time I read this psalm. "...They are like trees planted by streams of water..." I feel like whoever the originator of this name -- possibly the Germanic tribesmen who first placed the title on his son -- thought something similar. Perhaps they were some of the first Germanic converts to Emperor Constantine's new Christian state religion.

There is a small chance that the name was passed out after the conversion of the Roman empire. That some Germanic tribe had heard this psalm. there were after all proselytizers even in the 4th century, and the inherent goodness of it struck him. Or, that trees planted by streams are inherently and universally recognized as something good and wonderful and lovely, and also strong and secure.

As any Goth or ancient Roman Christian, or psalmist, or prophets know, trees planted by rivers and streams thrive. Even in times of drought, when even the river itself may dry up and no longer flow, there is a deep wetness, a soaked-ness, to the river bed and all the surrounding ground. Roots that run deep into the bank of a river stay soaked with water even when other fields run dry.

It was certainly something that resonated with Jeremiah's audience. This line is an echo of what we read in Jeremiah 17:8, which goes into great detail of the health of roots that are dug into floodplain soils and lack of fear they have in bearing fruit through the dry seasons.

Trees planted by water actually transpirate more water into the air. This makes it cooler as the moisture is wicked into the atmosphere. In large volume, this creates a breeze as the transpiration of the upper branches creates a subtle pull to groundwater in its own process of evaporation. In a very real way, trees planted by water change the environment around them.

But, enough history and science.

Because this is a lesson on basic things, isn't it? In our summer series, we are going back to the basics of our faith and looking to the most common, the most fundamental concepts and verses that guide our faith.

And what is more fundamental than this image:
Plant a tree by the river.
Put your fields and groves on its banks.
If your livelihood depends on this food, sow by the streams.

It was something the ancients knew far before the Germanic tribes assigned my wife's family name.

All of this talk of water in the wake of our neighbouring states flood disaster seems in really poor taste. In WV the death toll from the flood is at about 30 people and still going up as reports come in. It's so bad over there that the Greenbrier Resort has opened its doors to flood victims. Thousands of people are without power, and hundreds have lost their homes.

Paul says that all things are working together for good, but to tell folks in the midst of tragedy to just "buck up" and things will work out is a poor theology. Likewise saying that our understanding of "good" is not the same as the Almighty's is wrong, because how could God create a people with a yearning in their hearts for goodness that is in contrast to the goodness of our universal Father?

Instead, this part of Chapter 8 in Romans feeds the same fire that Paul has been stoking this whole time. That God is trustworthy, and that God is in a covenant of faithfulness to God's people.

In Romans, Paul says that all of creation is groaning, straining and crying out in the pain that will bring something new. Not only creation, not only the whole world, not only everything that has been made, but we ourselves. The children, the people, our spirits -- crying and sweating and groaning. The whole of the church then has joined creation in this. The suffering church in Rome, the people of WV, of Florida, of this city. Paul says that our pain is not in vain; it is not empty weeping at the state of a world gone insane, but instead, they are labor pains. They are tears and sweat and gritted teeth that are bringing in something new.

And not only the created world and the church but also the Holy Spirit. The paraclete, that which Christ has sent for us, to be a helper and as Paul says to aid us in our weakness. The spirit groans as well because when Paul says, "all things work together for good," he is saying, not ONLY the things which I have just mentioned to you but all things.

That does not mean that the things we interpret as bad are really good. There are things that are heinous and wrong and unjust in this world. Paul is saying that the pain we have in the face of those things, the cry that we put out does not go unheard and for no purpose. But instead, those cries are birthing a renewed world. That God is faithful. That we are a large family of called and glorified people, and we are getting bigger all the time.

We are like a tree planted by a river.

We are not called to walk, stand, or sit in a way that would make us wicked, or sinful, or scoff at God. We are made to be planted. To root deeply; to bear out droughts and create fruit and new life.

The psalm ends in, well, in a way that might seem harsh I suppose. The last word is "perish," just as the first word is happy -- and if you know these Hebrew authors you know that was on purpose. The word "happy" begins with the first letter of the Hebrew alphabet and the word for "perish" begins with the last. From "A to Z," this psalm is complete. All you need in life, the "cliff notes" of what's to come after.

But this line about perishing -- it's not a prophecy. It's not a "just you wait and see." It's a gardener's note. It says if you cut off your source... if you plant yourself elsewhere.... if you try and live and bear fruit without water... you will die.

In essence, if you think you can do this thing called existence without the sustenance found in God, you'll die.

Listen to the stream. The coolness of the air. The community of rustling leaves in the trees. Close your eyes in the peace of, and feel the fundamental basic nature of the happiness that resides there. Don't cut yourself off. Don't try it alone. Don't think your labor, your groaning, your sweat, are for nothing.

Be delighted. Yield fruit. And do not wither.

8
Jesus Can't Stand the In-Laws Either

Written during our Thanksgiving celebration of worship after the 2016 election

EZEKIEL 18:21-25
LUKE 14:15-26

It's that time again.

More often, I have heard stories about families who are not particularly looking forward to the Thanksgiving holiday and the time with their families. There are stressors involved that go beyond finding a place for everyone to sleep and running out of coffee at just the wrong time. Everyone works hard to savor the moments we get as family, driving through endless traffic, negotiating lines in the shopping markets, cooking dishes at a volume and level of expertise that isn't what we are used to. Creating place settings. Getting out the kids table. Negotiating the various food sensitivities. We are basically creating the perfect storm for trouble even in the best of years. Surely this isn't the Kingdom of God. We do it because we want to be thankful. We want to honor what we have and be together with the people that mean the most to us in the world and resonate with that feeling of thanks. To appreciate each other. To appreciate our lives. It doesn't always work out as we have moments of friction, but that is the intent.

In Ephesians, Paul calls the church the "bride of Christ," and like any bride we come with our own families. Like every family, that means that we have in-laws as well, or rather that kind of makes us all in-laws of each other.

Now given the title, you might be a little nervous about where this is going, but maybe "can't stand the in-laws" was a little dramatic. In reality, like the in-laws of our social structure, when Jesus comes into our celebrations, we come to the party like in-laws. As people that are there celebrating with the family as those who have married in. We are there by covenant, and not by blood. Someone made a promise, and so we, by tradition and law, are part of this new family now. We come from a different country, we have traditions, needs and anxieties that Jesus Christ doesn't share.

When my wife and I got married there were a lot of traditions that we didn't share naturally with each other. A few years into our marriage we had a counselor tell us that we were, in fact, people from different countries who were coming together. We had different languages, in that we were used to talking about things in our own families - we had never known anything else really. We had different social expectations, different celebration rituals, different travel rules. It was incredible to have someone tell us all this. For me, it changed how I took things for granted and made assumptions about what was "normal" or to be expected in our new household that we were forging together.

That's what we are to Christ. People from an altogether different land trying to know the customs in this new celebration with our in-laws.

There are plenty of times in the gospels that Jesus has an issue with his followers, this new batch of in-laws trying to figure into the new family dynamic. In Luke[10] Jesus calls them foolish and slow of heart to their face. Talk about words that would start something at the dinner table! In Mark he is constantly telling them hush up[11], and you can feel a sense of Jesus' head shaking at intervals throughout the story. How much of a chance do we have if even the apostles themselves had a tough time getting to know the ways of the new family?

I have to give them credit though, the followers of Christ engaged well and made mistakes. Often enough, we brush up against one another in tension and quietly simmering arguments that have gone on for decades. We skirt issues at mealtimes under the guise of keeping the peace, and in doing so we miss the real story of what is going on. I'm not advocating brawls at every turn. There is a way to engage across divisions in our understandings or perspectives while still loving the people across from us. We have lost this valuable skill of listening to one another without having to convince the other person that our perspective is right.

Which brings to mind this question: Why do we care what the in-laws think? Or family in general? Why do they care what we think? Why couldn't we either live in a place where we could be unabashedly who we are, sharing the changes that happen in our lives with care, or why couldn't we just be truly happy and content to let anyone believe anything they think without challenge -- no matter how harmful or painful that belief may be?

I have a good friend who notoriously gets into something with his dad and grandfather at every visit. As he has grown up, the nature of those back and forths have changed, from the hot anger of youth to the more practised glowering discussions punctuated by explosions when one side or another has tried to be "civil" for too long. We've talked about how things have gone in the aftermath, and I came to the very sweet conclusion:

He engages them, and they him, because of their deep love.

It's not profound, but it is possibly something we don't always realize. We don't argue as much with people who aren't family, because we can blow

---

[10] Luke 24:25
[11] Mark 8:27-30

them off. The people we love are the ones who usually take the brunt of our passions. We get "into it" with family about the things we believe because we aren't satisfied with letting them think about things that we consider harmful.

Regardless of which position, no one argues because they *don't* care.

If the topic is seen as important, then it has to be engaged. To do less would be unloving.

Which is why Jesus engages with us at the dinner table.

This story from Luke is stark.

It's the story of a banquet thrower, a party-giver, an inviter to the table, who has their invitation rebuffed. The parable follows a comment that Jesus hears on how blessed it is to eat with Jesus. It must have been said sarcastically, or with the wrong inflection revealing what was really in their hearts, because the parable doesn't have a lot of good things to say. The meal has been tense so far. Jesus is eating in the house of a Pharisee and has already been quizzed and grilled. This parable shuts down further conversation.

Jesus wants the people eating at this table to understand something profound.

It is an un-righting of the world that the Pharisees believe they live in. There are rules and education and practices that have to be met to be a Pharisee. You are the elite if you are one of them, and Jesus, as a local celebrity is invited to the table. Jesus tells them however, they are going to miss out on the real food. If you let your own stuff get in the way of what God has prepared for you - even with all your wealth and knowledge and right practices - your place at the table will be given away. The people in the parable are all doing things that are good, things that should take precedent against a banquet according to all the rules that the Pharisees are comfortable with. A wedding. Your livelihood in crops. A new team of oxen. These are deeply cultural held icons of things that need to be done. Things that cannot wait. Still, their place at the table is given to anyone. Just anyone off the street. No chosen people. No place of honor reserved for particular people. Just anyone at all. There is a dire warning there. The house *will* be full. Whether or not you are a part of that, is up to you. Choose your own path, your own understanding of the rules, and you won't get to eat.

Notice that this isn't the first plan. The host had people in mind. People who were called to be there. Since they couldn't get out of their own way, an alternative was created. This later result is because of the actions of those who refused.

It's the same story in Ezekiel. God is having a conversation about what people do. It's not their station in life, or their family's exploits. Life isn't dependent on what your parents did or didn't do - it isn't even dependent on what you have done in the past. Instead it is about what you *are* doing. The choice you are making right now. To follow the Lord or not. To join in the feast or not. In Ezekiel we learn that Ezekiel is set as a watchman for the people of Israel, but, like the host throwing the banquet, God tells Ezekiel that no one is going to listen to him[12].

The message is not easy. In this reading and elsewhere the message is that God's people need to hear the signal of the watchman (the prophet) and repent. That they aren't going to coast by on good graces or on places of honor that they think they have earned. The death that people face will be on their own heads. Notice that death in this case isn't a punishment - it's simply a result. There is no life without the Lord. So, anything that happens, any kind of existence without God is a walking death. God doesn't want to see people turn away. It breaks God's heart. But if people make that choice, then spiritual death is the only result. God's goodness demands that the house be filled for the feast. Real choices have to be made. Real change has to be forged.

Why does God do this? Why does Jesus give this dire parable to the Pharisees?

In Ezekiel there are 2 kinds of hearts: the hardened hearts of those who will not listen, and the new heart of Israel found in those who will repent. As I said, it breaks God's heart for people to choose death. So, God engages with the people. Jesus, sitting at the table with people who have varying degrees of contempt and hate for him tells a strong story about choices. Because God loves people. Because God and Christ are not satisfied to allow us to continue to believe harmful things that lead us on a path to death.

As we go to our meals or our family gatherings over the next few days and gather around succulent birds cooked to perfection, and the side dishes that people have been making over and over for years until they are just right, set something in your heart as a watchman for the invading army, for the assault that is probably coming. When that watchman cries out, hear the love that is behind this perceived attack. Know that this person, like God, is talking like this because they aren't satisfied to let you continue as you are. In the anxiety of it all, there is an invitation to you. A feast that they think they have prepared in love.

It's enormously hard to do this. We have a field that needs tending. Family weddings to plan. Oxen that need to be broken in. But hear the invitation, and know that Jesus also has trouble with his in-laws. You are in good company. It comes from a place of love. Sometimes, yes, our family hurts us, like that army coming down the hill, destroying the city and taking the people of Ezekiel to Babylon. Sometimes their message of love is twisted up in their own brokenness and trauma. But don't let the face of the army make you forget who these folks are.

There is room at the table. Room for us all to be crippled and blind. Room for us to sit next to our family, who are also crippled and blind. Room

---

[12] Ezekiel 12:1-3

for us all to be poor in spirit and to have patience. This is how we see the feast that God sets for us.

So get ready for the big meal. The greatest blessing of all is to be at the banquet, as a family together.

9

The Incarcerated Church

ZECHARIAH 9:10-17
MATTHEW 25:31-46

The book of Acts is an incredible story of the first days of the ancient church and still has a directed and pointed message to the modern church as well. Of course, there is much we can learn, and the power of scripture still speaks to us in the same holy spirit language that it did in those days. Socially there is much that we share with the early church, as it was affected by religious zealotry and misunderstanding and the effects of idol worship and empire -- just as we are today.

As you read the book of Acts you can see the Holy Spirit at work in the church restoring and resurrecting, causing disruption and disturbance, establishing leadership, calling martyrs, performing miracles, and creating paths through which they and we could love our enemies.

There is one final realization to make about the book that is very important and often overlooked. It is necessary to understand this in order to really get what the author of Acts and the gospel of Luke was trying to accomplish. That is, that the whole story of the Holy Spirit is one that is tied to the idea of incarceration. It is that realization that is being communicated to the ancient church and our modern family.

First let's look at Luke's primary book, the Gospel, which focused on the human interactions and relationships of Christ. "Son of Man" is used as much in no other Gospel, and only in Luke do we realize that the woman bathing Christ's feet in oil[13] is *"hamartōlos"* that is, someone guilty of a crime, someone who is still "wicked." Only in Luke do we see conversations with thieves on the cross. Only in Luke does Jesus tell Zacheus[14] that Christ's purpose was to come and "seek and save the lost." Knowing this, it should come as no surprise that the book of Acts, Luke's second book, is also mainly concerned with how the church treated one another. It is again the story of human interaction that drives the narrative through the many initial structures and events of this burgeoning faith, this new way of being faithful, that the world had never seen before.

---

[13] Luke 7:36-50
[14] Luke 19:1-10

We know from Paul in Colossians[15] that Luke is a gentile, so it is no wonder that the way in which the church opened itself to the people who were once thought of as abhorrent and unclean, should be a passionate focus. Also, if we notice in the gospel of Luke, there is an elegantly written subtext. Luke, an educated gentile, is no stranger to literature and employs those same techniques if we are able to see them. The Gospel begins and ends with birth. In Chapter one, immediately after an introduction, we have the heralding, the foretelling, of John the Baptist and Jesus Christ. To end his first book, Luke concludes with the heralding of the church, yet still to be born in the book of Acts, as they are at the Jewish temple praising God, not yet in the fullness of what the Church would be. Luke is a fan of this style of writing.

So, as we finish Acts, what I see is another similar bookending. In Chapter 2, the followers of Christ are in one room. An upper room, after having concluded the business of electing a new person to replace Judas, they have no further direction. They are waiting. Isolated. In essence, locked away. Other Jewish folks are celebrating *Sha-vu-ot*, the Jewish name for Pentecost, the 50th day after Passover. Yet the followers of Christ were not. Shavuot should have them reading from the Hebrew Bible, and hanging greens, and harvesting wheat. Yet they sit together, incarcerated. But the story of the church arrives in full force driving them out into the world and to the ends of the earth. Similarly, at the end of Acts, we have Paul, the creator of the widespread church and the gentiles coming to an understanding of what it was to have a community, to have faith, to have an interwoven love and dependence, Paul is heading to prison. The story of Acts, this incredible fiery event. This legacy of the church that is found in the death of faithful people unwilling to recant their belief, this painful story of sacrifice and terror, this earth altering explosion of a belief that was passionately caring for people who had nothing. It ends with the incarceration of Paul in Rome. In four years Paul would be dead.

We might well ask what the ancients thought of prison, because it was different from what we have now. Largely in the time of the Old Testament, prisons were simply underground dungeons or empty wells. Think back to Joseph who was imprisoned by his brothers. They were wholly dark and miserable places. Jeremiah was put in "a cistern house" for many days. When he was let go for interrogation, he begged that he not be returned to his cell, afraid that he would die there. The psalmist several times writes of "prisoners in misery and in irons", captives who "groan" and are "doomed to die". Job considers Sheol to be the better choice for imprisonment, if we recall. Things were no better in Jesus' era. For the most part, the Roman prisons were dark, disease-ridden, and overcrowded. It was very common for prisoners to die in custody, either from disease or starvation, brutal torture, execution, or

---

[15] Collosians 4:14

suicide. In accounts, ancient historians and authors refer to prisons as a "fate worse than death."

So why is Luke using these themes in Acts? Not because of what prisons were, or only partly that, but because prisons serve principally as holding tanks where offenders could be detained prior to trial or to the carrying out of the sentence of the court, such as execution, exile or enslavement, or until debts or fines had been paid. Prison is where they waited, for debts to be paid. Much like the early church is waiting on the day of Pentecost. And how in Ephesians 3:1, Paul describes himself as a "prisoner of Christ" for the sake of the gentiles. Incarcerated in a fairly miserable place, expecting execution, yet working until the debt of the world was paid. That's Paul's understanding of being a prisoner. That the debt of the world needed to be paid in exchange for his freedom, and not just paid because Paul did believe that of course, but known. Even as a prisoner, Paul was serious about going after the least of these.

Many Christians in the early church languished in prison, awaiting their sentencing. Mostly because in the ancient secular world, that is everyone else, Jews and Gentile pagans, could not understand the new Christian belief systems. It was for the non-Christian, as the famous Churchill saying goes, "a riddle, wrapped in a mystery, inside an enigma."

The ancient world had never seen anything like this before. Which follows, since Jewish leaders had never seen anything like Jesus as a teacher before, and since we know the singular uniqueness that Christ has in all the universe. The ancient world didn't have regular communal meetings. The ancient world was not so inspired by their faith that they sought to draw others into their beliefs. The ancient world largely didn't have a system of belief, but instead just a loose gathering of ritual practices tied to family gods, city gods, and gods of the ruling state. The ancient world did not find morality or the insistence to care for the sick and poor and fringe people of their society from their system of belief. There are letters written by governors of the Roman empire back and forth on what to do with these Christians, who, at different points, are accused of eating children, since we take part in consuming the flesh of God's son, and drinking blood, and of having incestuous unions, since we called each other brother and sister.

Again, the ancient world did not know what to make of Christians. The number of people who were cared for and communicated with kept growing, however, and this fantastic story ends with Paul preaching under the eye of Roman guards, pleading his death sentence with the Emperor of the world.

There is a difference in Act's bookends of incarceration. Just as the expectation of the birth of two babies is different from the expectation of the fullness of the Church while worshipping at the Temple, this incarceration post - "Holy Spirit" is vastly different from the one we see at the beginning of Acts. The church is imprisoned in fear and wonder at the future before the arrival of the Holy Spirit on Pentecost. But here Luke is explicit in telling us: Paul "proclaimed the kingdom of God and taught about the Lord Jesus Christ—with all boldness and without hindrance!" Incarceration at the end of Acts no longer holds the isolation and fear and weakness that it once held. Nothing in all the world can stop the Holy Spirit.

As we heard this liturgy this morning, inspired by the poems of incarcerated people, I hope we can connect a little bit more with the prisoner. I hope that we see with new eyes the view that Paul had on his own life. I hope that we can deepen our understanding of the book of Acts, as the story of the incarcerated church. We are still prisoners of Christ, willingly taking on this imprisonment to find true freedom. Absorbing the unstable and less than ideal conditions of Christianity so that we can minister with deep love to those who are sick, who are strangers in our land, who are thirsty, who ache to be invited in, who are hopeless and alone and in need of our visits.

To "do" for the least of God's people, we have to take on a portion of their stories in empathy. To truly hear Christ call people brothers and sisters, to hear the insistence of the divine family in those people who have no status. To give humanity back to people who have been dehumanized. To give our power over to those people in our family who have no power of their own. To be counted as sheep instead of goats. We are to be incarcerated. We *are* to know hopelessness at times. We *are* to know starvation and time in the darkness of the cistern.

Yet, we are not prisoners *without* hope. We are, and will continue to be, as Zechariah says, "prisoners *of* hope." In the Old Testament reading, God is going to set the prisoners free from the waterless pit, the cistern, the darkness that was without end. Luke's companion to Acts, the Gospel, spells out why Jesus is here. The Messiah that Zechariah's people longed for, has come. The very first thing that Jesus does publicly as an adult in the Gospel of Luke tells people that the Lord:

> "...has been anointed (Christ)
> to proclaim the good news to the poor.
> God has sent (Jesus) to proclaim freedom for the prisoners
> and recovery of sight for the blind,
> to set the oppressed free..."

That is the story of the Church in the book of Acts. For Luke, the ministry of Christ and the true and faithful "shepherding" of the Church, is to live into incarceration in the name of the One who comes to give freedom to those who are shackled in the cisterns of our world. If they are fearing for their lives, or simply dealing with the loss of loved ones, they are the same, and they are a part of a family. Our lives have been altered by Christ and will continually be altered by the work that we are drawn into. We will weep and be martyred but that will not stop us, because we will also do miracles and be set on fire by a mighty wind.

Because that is our story. The Holy Spirit has gotten a hold of us now, and even though we are imprisoned by our own short-sightedness and trauma or by the mightiest governance in the world, as Paul was in Rome, we will proclaim, "with all boldness and without hindrance."

This thing called Church, much like in ancient times, still seems like a crazy idea on a lot of days. If we truly desire the righteous eternal life, if we want to shine like jewels in the land, if we want to flourish and be full, then we must be prisoners. Incarcerated together in this work, knowing what real freedom looks and tastes like, and bringing that Good News to the ends of the earth.

10

How the Mighty have Fallen

Written as our faith community dealt with loss and separation

2 SAMUEL 1:25
ROMANS 8:18-25
EXODUS 7:14-11:10

So let's talk about Egypt.

During the book of Exodus, in the New Kingdom period, it was a military superpower. They had made incredible tech advances that were years ahead of any of their neighbors.

This is the time of the two-horse chariots which were the atom-bomb of the day. They were fast and scary--just having them emerge on the battlefield was sometimes enough to turn the tide. These were elite troops with incredibly powerful recurve bows that took two men to string.

This is the time of the *khopesh*, a fantastic military weapon that was light and agile and could pull down the shields of your enemies and open them up for quick attacks.

This is the advent of the state-owned, professional military in the ancient world. These soldiers were highly trained, battle-hardened and better than anyone else at what they did. Under Ramses II, the empire stretched from the Nile to Sidon and parts of Syria. They fought the Hittites in battles that involved tens of thousands of soldiers, an unheard of number at the time.

The Egyptian kingdom was enormous, ethnically unified, theologically supreme in their era, and governmentally and militarily superior to anyone else in the world.

And the Israelites needed to find a way to leave.

Luckily God had a plan for that.

In reality, the plagues that meet Egypt are a systematic decimation of the Egyptian war machine as well as a deconstruction of their theological and governmental structure. The plagues are not an upping of the ante in response to Pharaoh's stubbornness. They are literally carving a path for exit through an implacably strong war nation.

But let's get back to Pharaoh's stubbornness.

If we recall the conversation that Moses and God have back at the burning bush, God knows what the outcome is going to be. "I will harden his heart" is more literally "I will strengthen his heart." The Hebrew *khä·zak'* means a fortifying of sorts, the kind that we would regularly understand to be beneficial, the kind of thing we pray for in the midst of tragedy when we hear of brothers and sisters entering into hard times. I will pray for strength. That's what God is doing for Pharaoh.

Because the plagues aren't a reaction. They are a calculated military and spiritual move, and God needs Pharaoh not to relent until the last plague has taken its toll, until the whole message has been heard. God is extricating the Isrealite people from the people of Egypt and the message has to be clear.

Consider then, the plagues.

The first plague creates thirst in all the land. Even wells that are dug are undrinkable. Salty, irony, and putrid bloody water. The maximum a human can go without water is about a week. That means conservative movement, not going out in the sun, and still getting some moisture from foods. Dehydration is serious and causes things like fainting, swollen joints, cramping, seizures and difficulty breathing. Imagine that any available moisture went to the ruling class and the army, and that there was almost certainly not enough to go around. The first plague wasn't a magic show. It was a death sentence.

So we see the plagues are not escalating as Pharaoh is made more stubborn. This isn't a fight between the will of man and the will of God. God has already won at the first stroke. The plagues are filled with death at every moment, and Pharaoh is given the strength by God to endure them. Because the message has to be finished.

People are hallucinating, recovering from nausea, vomiting, cramping, migraines, and this is *as a nation*. This was an epidemic. And just as there is some relief, there are thousands of frogs everywhere.

To really *get* this plague you have been an Egyptian. There was a goddess in their pantheon, Heqet, who was frog-headed. She was the goddess of fertility, as you can imagine, so named after seeing the yearly spawn of frogs erupt from the River Nile's banks. But now, frogs are everywhere. In the bread, in the beds, in the jars, in the wells, in the fields, in the barns... This is a theological attack. The Egyptian gods are breaking down. The natural theological expectation is being undone by this God of the Israelites. Because of the holy status of the frogs, they were not killed. But as they died, their corpses were heaped into sticky piles.

The government has been shut down. People have died by the droves. Nothing is getting done. Pharaoh relents for a time -- how could he not! But God fortifies him, and the Israelites are brought back. Because the message is not finished.

Then the bugs came. The Hebrew, *ken,* is a little vague on what exactly these bugs are. Some say lice, some say gnats, a better translation would be "the swarm." The swarm in your face, in your hair, their larvae are in your food... And so again, no work can be done in the land.

Ever walk through a cloud of gnats? Imagine that *all* the time.

Fields are going fallow, there is no medical aide, no city works, no garbage collection, no couriers, no payments going out, more importantly - the war arm of the empire is not being taken care of. The highly technological bows that required almost daily care. Care which cannot be maintained. Not to mention that the army is suffering along with everyone else. Loss of life is everywhere.

In the next plague the animals suffer and die. In a lot of depictions we see cows and goats laying down. And that's true, but usually we do not see the most important aspect to this plague. The horses. The highly trained and prized Egyptian thoroughbreds. The chariot pullers. The integral piece of the war machine. All dying by the hundreds.

Never mind the effect of the rest of these plagues on the general public, think of the effect on the troops. Boils means your skin is so scarred and raw that no armor will be worn. Hail means that all of your fields, the fruit trees and vines for wine and vinegar, the herbs are broken and destroyed. Wine was taken as a preservative along with vinegar on long campaigns, and herbs were the source of Egyptian medicine. So that means no long military campaigns which would need medics. No healthcare system for anyone at all.

Locusts eat the last of the food, and the production system is already decimated. The army faces starvation. They can't grow their own food -- they are professional soldiers. Those who are supposed to be growing it on their behalf are almost completely wiped out.

Then comes the darkness. Egyptians had gods for everything, and they have been failing with each plague that came along. And now: the last and most powerful god, Ra, has lost. The eternal Ra, the Sun god, the place from which the Pharaoh's power comes. Defeated in utter darkness. Obliterated.

And finally Death. This last plague is clear. The time of Egypt is over. Your heirs are no more. There is nothing left for you, once-great nation of this world. In under a year, this power that has lasted for thousands of years was essentially over. Only God's people have a future.

Egypt never recovers.

History shows the following years would be ones of constant war, with a newly arisen "Sea People" who mercilessly exhausted Egypt's troops, and after they were finally repelled by Ramses III, old enemies and internal conflict finished killing the Egyptian Empire. It lay basically in its death throes until the Greeks and then the Romans came to put them out of their misery ages later.

The plagues were a systematic destruction of everything the Egyptians thought to be true.

The scene at the Red Sea should take a different tone, in light of the plagues.

This was not the Egyptian war machine coming to get the Israelites who were thundering down from the mountains. These were the last living troops. The remnant. They are starving. They have no medicine. No horses. No armor. Their health is gone. Their robustness has evaporated. Their faith is shaky. Their lineage is cut off. They are soldiers without peace. They are grey-headed, sunken-eyed, echoes of the men they once were. Who have watched their sons and neighbors die by the hundreds. They are weeping and weak. Egypt is destroyed before they ever even try and follow Israel across the sea.

Fifteen percent of the entire book of Exodus is devoted to the plagues. Somehow this is important to the theology that these new believers in God Almighty are meant to take with them. Could you imagine witnessing this tragedy, unharmed, for almost a year? God took care of these wayward children like no other point in history. God destroys a nation to provide for their escape, God leads them with fire and cloud, parts the sea for them, feeds them daily, and springs fresh water from the desert rocks. God provides for their *every* need and protection. How did this affect their expectations of God? How did this insert itself into their understanding of who God is?

Do you think the Israelites were surprised when they were later defeated and exiled by the Babylonians and the Persians?

Yet, we have this same sense today don't we? That we, the chosen people, are going to exist outside of the land of plagues and dwell only in the land of Goshen. A place free of blood and flies, where our animals are healthy, and our children surround us in perfect peace. That we as Christians are surely more blessed, and should be more blessed than non-believers. That we as Christians should be the most powerful people. Some Christians do think we should be the most wealthy people, and perhaps the best looking people on the face of the earth. We expect that. We do, and I know it because of the initial disbelief with which we meet our tragedy.

"Uh! My car got hit with a grocery cart!"

"Uh! My house was flooded!"

"Uh! My spouse was diagnosed with cancer."

There is a sense that we can't believe it could happen to us. From the silly to the honestly tragic, we have this hubris in us. Born out of an expectation of blessing.

We might expect to live in Goshen, but that is not our reality.

Our reality is that we, like the later Israelites, exist in the time of captivity and plague, of sickness and death, of persecution and injustice.

I don't deal well with tragedy. Honestly, I expect life in Goshen like it's some kind of deal that God and I have worked out ahead of time. Something like, I will work eagerly and diligently for God's will and justice in this world, and I get to cruise through being sheltered and taken care of and mostly joyful. But there is no such deal.

So how in the world do we live without hubris and expectation and still find hope enough to live each day?

Paul tells us that the whole world, every part of creation joins us in life on the other side of Goshen. We are all, every fiber and atom of the created universe groaning out in pain at what the universe *is*. And this pain, this Greek word *synodino*, is a pain that *all* share. If you are a good Presbyterian, you may hear a familiar word buried in that - Synod - our word for the collection of presbyteries, which is simply Greek for assembly, or meeting. It shares a root to this word and is being used in regard to the type of pain that Paul expresses as a "pain for the assembly." All who are here, together, we feel this. And that's where Paul finds the hope that Egypt never had.

Though Egypt was unified as a culture and as a people, they were not unified in their theology. New gods came and went, old gods were blended into new ones, temples rose and were rededicated, and the whims of the gods seemed to shower favor and take it away arbitrarily. The ruling classes were under no compunction to share power, or initiate a sense of justice, and the suffering of one population in their group was not felt by the others. The Israelites' issues as slaves went uncared for by the Egyptians. They were a people, each of them, alone.

These new people in Acts and who then are reading Paul's letters, these Christians, have a different take. We are together. We bear the pain of one another; we feel the suffering together, and even beyond that all of God's creation is in line with us. We are joined together as brothers and sisters, and creation and created beings, in an unbroken and expectant movement that waits in our suffering for liberation.

That is the power of God's people. That is the power we have to see beyond the present tragedy and into a hopeful future. Not by having singular strength. But by sharing the pain together.

We read this passage in Romans incorrectly. We read that Paul doesn't want to complain about the world's current woes, because he compares them to the world to come. We take that to mean that we should grit our teeth and muscle through the current pains in our lives and just keep hanging on until the wonderfulness of the world to come arrives.

That's not what Paul actually says. In our desperation for the personal independence of American self made strength, we read right over this wonderful beautiful plural first-person objective pronoun: us. In Greek *hēmas*. We together, us, all of us, are going to manifest this Glory. *Hemas* is the direct object of that phrase, so this isn't heaven that Paul is talking about. It's us. You and me, brothers and sisters, all of creation. It's groaning. Waiting desperately for us to adopt each other.

We have to move beyond asking for strength to whether this life of plague and tragedy is our reality. Being strong enough to go through something isn't enough, and apparently, according to Pharaoh it can have a dark side. God can make us strong. But Paul is seeing a new way in the book of Romans. He is encouraging us into a better mode, a mode that has weakness and not strength at its core. A way of being that shares our strife, that feels the pain of this world together and in that sharing in that togetherness, in that glorious *us* we find a hope heretofore unrevealed in the world.

God destroys a nation to convey something. God does it to convey the very thing that Paul is talking about here in his letter to the Romans. This word: Hope, in the Greek *elpitzo*. And beyond hope, as we hear it translated here, it has another meaning. Trust. In Exodus God is making introductions to the children of Israel, and the first thing God shows them is how far God will go to earn their trust. Almost a year dismantling the most powerful force on earth. Another generation caring for them and watching over them in the wilderness. This message: Trust me. Set your hope on Me. And Paul, who knows this Exodus lesson, is saying that we find this hope in one another.

We are in fact saved by this hope. We are saved from a life of solitude, and perhaps a life of singular strength that serves only to isolate us. We are saved from a life of singular pain and are instead living a life of hope in the midst of this place of plagues. The epidemic of life that we are called to live, not as singular people but as a people of faith together.

And that changes our hubris. It changes our expectations and our entitlement as Christians.

My husband has cancer; my daughter died; my baby isn't safe here; my sister won't stop drinking.

Our response changes from one of indignation to one that expects tragedy, shares this pain, and finds a saving hope. Something that Paul admits can be elusive. His encouragement is not something that he says we already possess, but something that we pursue, and that we expect *fully* (*apekdechomai*) to come to pass. We are called, in the midst of this plague-ridden world to form a place of hope and trust together. Not a place that exists without hurt or pain, but a place where we together are adopted into each other's lives. Not as something that we will continually already have, but as something we will faithfully work for and fully expect to come to pass in the future.

That place that is only found together. That place of hope and trust in God which is the glory that is revealed in us. Only together can we get there. Only together do we survive the plague.

11
Sabbath as Healing

JOHN 5:1-15
2 SAMUEL 24:11-17

Growing up whenever I was sick there were a few things that I knew I could expect, and would even look forward to, as I felt myself getting ill. Cheese muffins and tomato soup.

Okay, that might not sound so great, but there was something so comforting about these things, one made by my mom and the other, a speciality of my dad.

I have no idea how or why my mom started making cheese muffins, which is just an English muffin, smothered in butter, with a few slices of plain old American cheese on it, which you then toast in the oven, or a toaster. It was so warming and comforting, really both dishes were. My dad's Syrian tomato soup was heavy with rice and cinnamon and pepper, and as you ate it you could feel restoration coming to you.

There is something nice about being sick. Especially as a kid, but even as an adult, even if you don't have someone to come and wait on you, there can be a healing permission that we give ourselves when we are sick to be restful that lends a certain kind of comfort. Of course this has to be the right kind of sick to really enjoy it. You have to be perhaps on the upward swing of recovery, that feeling of tiredness without the racking cough or emergency sprint to the bathroom. No one can enjoy that kind of sickness. But in that sweet spot, where we can call off our obligations, take a sick day, surround ourselves with comfort food and binge-watch our favorite show without any sense of guilt, there is something glorious about it.

I remember sitting in bed as a kid, warm in my blankets, the spicy steam coming off a bowl of soup, and a favorite book propped up in front of me. The crunch of that buttery English muffin, and the gooey cheese sticking just slightly to the roof of my mouth. There can be something nice about being sick.

Being sick can also be very isolating.

Every time we have an outbreak of Hand, Foot and Mouth disease here at the church preschool, they put a sign on the doors letting parents know and of course staff and other people in the building. When I see it, I usually run a mental checklist in my head about the things that I could accomplish outside the office instead. When I am inside there is a marked difference in how I enter and act with the kids in the hallway too, ever thinking, "Is this one of the infected, or soon to be? What's the incubation carrier period again for this?" Heaven help you if you see that sign on a day when the church staff hosts a chapel session for our preschool kids. There are always hugs at the end of that for the leaders, and when there is an outbreak I unconsciously grimace and stiffen.

There are friends of ours who always warn us away when their kids are coming down with something, and it's a great courtesy, but it does invite a kind of isolation on the family.

When we adults get sick, and there isn't anyone immediately available to make us cheese toasts or tomato soup, we rely on our friend networks or church family, or just make do with the self-imposed or required isolation that being sick sometimes demands of us. It's almost a total flip in a lot of ways; as fun as it is to be sick as a kid sometimes, it is equally depressing and tedious to be sick as an adult. There have been several occasions that, during a hospital visit, folks have commented to me about the loneliness that comes with being hospitalized, and the great meaning that visits have, of course, to break up the "never alone, always lonely" feeling of being in medical care. You are surrounded by people taking care of you and can feel like you are literally never having a moment's peace to yourself, yet still be terribly lonely in the midst of all that hustle.

It's interesting to me that this is a point as well for the man sitting by the pool from our reading in John. It's an easy thing to overlook, but factors heavily into a big part of the meaning of the passage.

Verse 5 begins the conversation between Jesus and a man who has been there seeking to be healed by the waters for thirty-eight years. Scripture says that Jesus learns this, so we can assume that they have been chatting a little bit on this Sabbath day. Jesus finally asks the Jesus questions, which seems to us very normal having read a lot about Jesus, it is something that we expect Jesus to say, the question, "Do you want to be healed?"

I love the response because it is total sarcasm which we know was a part of not only the ancient Greek media of the day in the form of their Satyr comedies but also a deeply entrenched tradition of the Israelite faith story. Remember Elijah[16] standing around the "offering competition" with the priests of Ba'al? He encourages them to pray louder for a sign to consume their offering by saying, "Maybe your god is just sleeping." Total sarcasm.

Knowing that, and imagining that these statements and questions from our reading today are taking place within a larger conversation that Jesus and the man have been having, I re-imagine this, complete with British accent by Eric Idle, to play out like this: "Look, My Lord, Dinnit you hear me say I've

---

[16] 1 Kings 18:20-40

been here for thirty-eight years? Do you see anyone around who is going to carry me down? Yeah, I try to get down there but some other geezer gets ahead of me, big surprise, and gets healed instead. Do I want to be healed? Are you having a laugh?" I don't know why I imagine an accent, it just feels like this guy by the pool is being played by Eric Idle or something.

In the original Greek, the response is still sarcastic, and even in English we can see that this isn't the resounding "Yes Lord!" response that we expect. I mean, who is this guy? I imagine that Jesus laughs though, chuckling at him in a way that says, "Okay, maybe you're right, of course, you want to be healed, and you've been here a long time." And so, of course, the story goes on and Jesus heals him.

Laced in that sarcasm, is a vulnerable admission, especially for someone that was a Jew in the ancient world. "I have no one to help me get into the pool." For thirty-eight years, there has not been one person who would help this man. Not a family member, or a friend, or someone he grew up with at the synagogue. No one. For thirty-eight years. This is his isolation of illness. Year after year. Isolated. Cut off, and alone. This is a community that is built on the understanding of being a whole people together. The only ones who are cut off in that Torah understanding are the ones who are not following the Law. They are outside the community, and suffer a total loss of identity. We can commiserate, those of us who have known people who struggled through chronic illness.

So when Jesus offers to heal him, this man, literally, jumps at the chance and goes out on his merry way. Which brings us to another part of this healing that is so strange. Not only do we have this odd sarcastic reply to Jesus, but also, as we find out later, this guy had no idea who it was that healed him. Later the religious police also had no idea who this man was who had been healed (though he has been at the pool for thirty-eight years - a real testament to the isolation he's been experiencing). They aren't amazed that he is walking around after more than three decades; they don't rejoice with him at his walking; they are just concerned that he is carrying his mat on the Sabbath.

There is a whole separate missing miracles sermon there that we can save for another day.

This is another serious moment for the healed man.

Right now, being healed, he has a chance to rejoin the community, his Jewish family, his sentence in prison is over. However, because he was healed on the Sabbath, his healing breaks Jewish law code and runs the risk of pushing him right back outside the community again.

The ancient people in the time of Christ valued and held their own worth in three things as a Jewish person: being circumcised, obeying purity laws and observing the Sabbath. This is their whole identity, and so in a totally rational moment of, "I'm not going back to being alone" moment, the healed man throws Jesus under the bus. "Hey, it's not my choice, this guy who healed me told me to do it." Oh, healed you, you say? On the Sabbath? Tell us more...

Which brings us to another odd layer of this event.

Why heal on the Sabbath?

It would have been the easiest thing in the world to tell the guy that you were coming back tomorrow, or better yet, just sit with him until sundown. There is no burning building that he is lying in. The waters of the pool aren't threatening to flow over his head, and he has been there for thirty-eight years already! It's not especially loving, because healing him on the Sabbath ends up making more trouble for the guy. It makes no sense on all sides, why Jesus would choose to do this on the Sabbath. Moreover, Jesus specifically tells the guy to take his mat with him, an obvious act on the Sabbath that would be immediately discovered. He could have healed him quietly and told him to leave it. But Jesus doesn't do that. It causes trouble, makes waves, and is totally not necessary.

And that is the point.

Jesus sets that up when he sees that man again later. Scripture is sure to point out to us that he sees him at the temple, worshiping with the body of believers, again part of the covenant family, and even goes further to say, "See? You are healed. Stop sinning."

The sin *is* the unbelief. The man doesn't, or hasn't, "known" Jesus this whole time. That's the worst thing, living a life in the darkness of not knowing Jesus. It's not a threat, let's be clear, this isn't Jesus hanging the sword of Damocles over his head. This is the statement of truth. You were healed, you can't go back to who you used to be, that would be a terrible thing.

The point is the *new thing*. The fresh wine that is coming in that cannot be held in the new wineskins. This is who Jesus is. No part of the old system can be allowed to permeate the new way. If Jesus had waited until after the Sabbath was over, or just let the healed man leave his mat, the statement would have been that some parts of the old system were still going to work in the New Kingdom that was coming to fruition through Christ's life, death and resurrection. And the fact is, that they aren't. Trying to elide the old systematic understanding of oppression into the new world that Jesus made wasn't going to work. To do so would be sin, and the "worse thing" that Jesus talks about.

Our reading from the Old Testament relates a story of God healing the people that were being punished for David's sin. David couldn't trust God and instead wanted to trust the might of his own self, and that's not who God is. So God corrects that behavior with punishment, and receives a costly sacrifice from David as the payment for his lack of trust and failure as a leader. That world and that the understanding of who God is just won't work in the Kingdom that Christ is building.

Jesus Christ doesn't require anything from the man he heals by the waters that day. He doesn't even require that the man know his name, or have even the basic understanding of his station as rabbi or prophet or Son of God since the healed man refers to Jesus simply as "the man." There are no prior criteria, there is no sacrificial requirement, there is only healing, and a strong warning about the paths that lead to life, and the paths that lead to death.

Jesus isn't making it easy for people to believe and is going about the work of reshaping the corrupted faith system of these folks in Jerusalem without leaving them an out. Jesus even doubles down with the Jewish authorities when they confront him about his transgression saying "Not only did I heal on the Sabbath, but I did it because I'm the Son of God." That's like getting into trouble and then telling your parents that you also did a worse thing. "Yeah, I borrowed the car without asking Dad, but I did it while blindfolded and with a case of beer in the back for my underage siblings."

Jesus cites that God and Christ both work on the Sabbath because of who they are, and it's only later in John that Jesus specifies what the work is that he is talking about. Because this isn't Jesus flip-flopping on previous understandings of what Sabbath is, it's just a continued expression. In the next chapter of John, Jesus says that the work of God is to believe in the one that God has sent. The same thing he was telling the healed man at the temple.

That's the real work we do.

The expressions of our belief in Jesus Christ, and that Jesus is truly God incarnate. To be believed and believed in, to be sought after, to be heard, to be understood. Regardless if the message is hard on us to hear because we, like the Jewish authority, take issue with an aspect of Jesus' teachings in the way that it has manifested and required us to do something in our own life. Beware of the God who likes to double down. "Oh, you thought that was a tough concept that really shook your worldview and your understanding of who Jesus is? Well, just wait..."

The centrality of celebrating the Sabbath becomes our expression and understanding of who God is through Christ Jesus.

Spending time in worship, playing with family, truly resting, studying, volunteering, praying, healing; doing the things that Christ did. Loving each other, loving ourselves. Loving God. That's the best expression of Sabbath.

We are able to do it because we have been healed from our spiritual ailment of wrongness. The isolation of our souls has been broken by Grace and we are able to truly and more fully understand what the Sabbath holds for us. The way forward -- out of sickness -- is only experienced together so that no one can say, "I have no one." We are healed on the Sabbath, so that we may know and believe in our Lord.

12
Epigenetic Good News

Written after the start of the new year

LUKE 16:14-31
2 SAMUEL 12:1-10

Everyone is doing a year in review. Even my daughter's children's show, "Tru and the Rainbow Kingdom" did one, recounting the past adventures of previous episodes. For Tru and her pals, it was a big year. There was a magical creature who stunk so bad that they had to try three magical wishes just to try and contain the smell. Her cat, Bartlby, learned to be a ninja. The king of the kingdom made peace with his brother. Big things going on there.

We could do that for our churches as well. There might not be any ninjas being trained (although you never know with ninjas, which is kind of the point). I know a few pastoral colleagues that have even worked up a video, although even that is already done for us on Facebook and other social media sites. These review posts are consistently the most used and viewed auto-app that the sites create - across all age groups and generations. On the whole, people love a good recap episode.

I think I have to ask why we do that? We want to look back at the good we have done, and it feels good to do, sure. I think we also want to know the kind of story we are leaving in our wake. The review is a way of chronicling the good of the past in a way that can feel more permanent. This isn't the blooper reel, it's the highlights.

We want to know that what we leave behind is good.

We know we aren't going to live forever, so there is a part of us always thinking about the legacy we will leave behind, and the year in review is a little aspect of that. A check in, and a solid marker about our past.

When you think about your legacy, you might think about your wealth. Especially if you are nearing a retirement milestone, or have a child or two whom we imagine will either depend on or be blessed by our final estate.

It's strange that we think about that because scripture encourages us to do the opposite.

Jesus talks a lot about wealth. A lot. Jesus talked more about money than any other subject outside of the Kingdom of God. And especially in this chapter in Luke Jesus talked directly to the Pharisee about wealth and derided him for it. He calls the wealth of the world a wicked wealth or "false wealth" and talks about it being used as a test for the real wealth.

The idea that money is a test isn't new even in the time of Christ. Jesus is quoting from a well known passage in Deuteronomy 8:17-18;

"Otherwise, you may say in your heart, 'My power and the strength of my hand made me this wealth.' "But you shall remember the LORD your God, for it is He who is giving you power to make wealth, that He may confirm His covenant which He swore to your fathers, as it is this day."

The Pharisee knows this verse. Memoization of the Deuteronomical texts is step one on the path to being a Pharisee. The author of Luke even goes so far as to say that they loved money. Not God. Not the Law. But money. That is their orientation, and Jesus knows this and so entered into a teaching parable. For Jesus, we can see earthly wealth is a distraction, and a trial. It's not really a boone except possibly in that it leads to some kind of good legacy. But when the legacy of the wealth itself can become the focus, then we become corrupted ourselves. When our orientation is one of, "How will our wealth continue forever?" our hearts, known by God, become detestable in God's sight. That's a strong word. The Greek is *bdelygma*, a tough word for western mouths. It is also translated as "abomination, foul" and "idolatrous." It's a very strong word, and Jesus, through Luke's gospel, is applying this to all people who orient their lives around money.

Let's be clear here that there are a few ways that we can orient ourselves in this abominable way. Do we fret over the family inheritance? Are we fighting for our "fair" share? Do we sit on an endowment board that has forgotten its purpose in favor of gaining more capital? Are we struggling to make ends meet - and allowing ourselves to be consumed with worry? Do we make donations just shy of anonymity so that the grapevine reflects a little publicity back at us?

We can easily be consumed with our legacy of wealth, when in fact - our true legacy is Good News.

What's better: a check or grace? We equate money with freedom, and to a certain degree of meeting our needs that is true, but it is so easy to forget that real freedom only comes in Christ.

Instead of an inheritance of cash, we have the capability and the charge from Christ to change the DNA of what we send into the next generation. Like the man who is in *sheol*, we are responsible for what we leave behind, and after we are gone, our intentional influence on the world ends.

There is a discipline of biology called epigenetics, which is the study of alterations to genetic expression that doesn't involve changes to actual genetic coding. Think of things like smoking or diet altering the weight or size of our children.[17] The way we eat as children can in essence program our genes to expect a certain lifestyle later in our lives and can make us

---

[17] "Epigenetics Clues to Obesity and How Lifestyle Changes Could Modify Your Epigenetic Profile" by Estephany Ferrufino, *What is Epigenteics?*

predisposed to gaining or losing weight. You can notice trends in family systems also, in the ways that alcoholism, absenteeism, trauma, and anxiety all have a continued effect on the expectation and propensity of the body generations later.

Think of this in terms of our spiritual DNA as well. We can affect our core understandings and present different actions to the world outside of the structure with which we were born. If we really see ourselves as new creations in Christ, we may even imagine that our core structure should be remade as well. It is important to think about how we present our beliefs, the ways in which we are leaving a legacy to the next generation, what genes we are passing along as we review our previous year. Are we leaving behind a teaching of abomination or Good News?

It is easy to be blinded by our actions. Especially when we are powerful.

King David, one of the most beloved characters in all of scripture, does one of the most heinous things we could imagine.

For a little context on this passage about Nathan the prophet, let's run our own little pre-episode recap. David is king. He has won his victories in battle. He has suffered under King Saul, including the loss of his beloved Jonathan. For now, things are mostly stable, as some battles are still being fought, David has returned to the capitol. He is at the height of his power.

Then, as he is lecherously spying on a woman cleansing herself in her rooftop bath, he takes a dark turn. He desires her. As king, he calls for her to be delivered to his room. As king he sleeps with her, which, in this action, his power and their married status makes this more like rape and less like a torid affair. After sleeping with her, likely more than once, she becomes pregnant. So King David embarks on a long plan of deceit trying to get her husband to take credit for the baby. When that fails, David essentially has him killed. Leaving the woman, raped, abused, pregnant, and without the agency of her husband to protect her.

I've told an age appropriate version of this story to my daughter, and she had a really hard time not seeing David as the villian. The kicker to all of this is that David sees nothing wrong with what he has done. When the prophet comes to tell the King a parable tale about the abominable level of injustice in his Kingdom, David has no idea that he is the one at fault. David is powerful. Rich. Wealthy. When we become that kind of person, it is so hard to alter the DNA of that life.

We become entitled and privileged without ever even knowing it. We expect things to just be done in a certain way that makes sense, the most sense, to us. We can become the villians of a story by doing all the things it is legal for us to do. By doing things that are socially acceptable. By doing things that the world expects of us. Being wealthy isn't a sin. Loving money is an abomination.

David has to be told, as many of us might be, "You are the one!"

You are the one who has murdered and consumed this woman's life.

You are the one who has made your legacy detestable to God.

You are the one who refused to listen to God and the prophets.

Jesus' parable does not have a happy ending for the rich who have good things and easy lives on earth. The rich man lived in luxury every day. He ate good food and went out to eat. He traveled and never really had to save. He took just one vacation to Europe every year. The question wasn't *if,* but when and where. He wore purple linens. He had a nice car, and if it ever needed repairs, he repaired it without having to dip into savings. He had savings. He had equity. He had everything he or his children could ever need.

Yet, there was a beggar at his gate.

The placement of the beggar in this parable is important. This isn't someone from another city, or another region of the world. This was someone that the rich man passed by every day. Going in and out of the household he passed this man. Every day. The beggar's name, *Eleazar* in Hebrew, is important. It means "God has helped." In this story, it isn't the people who help this man as they have been instructed to do by God, it is instead only God who can help.

When humanity refuses or is too blind by their privilege to help, God will help. That's inspirational to the poor among us and a serious threat to we who are wealthy.

The end of this parable is an amazing turn of literary foreshadowing by Luke. What does Abraham tell the rich person in the last sentences? If they don't listen to Moses and the Prophets, they won't be convinced *even if* someone were to be raised from the dead.

If we can't listen to the work of the Old Testament, the Hebrew Bible, in regard to how we should disregard our own wealth in favor of equity for others. If we live in our plenty and cannot see the beggar at our doorstep then we certainly won't believe it when Jesus talks about it either, even though he came back from the dead. It goes beyond giving to the church. It goes beyond donating our time and money to other care organizations. It is our orientation to wealth. It is our conceptual notion that we deserve to have a car, or two. That we deserve to live in a house that is more than we need. That workers in our city who can't make a living wage is just the way it is. That people in our country go hungry, or cannot find good health care because it's just a big problem. It isn't about what percentage of our earnings we give it is about our concept of the purpose and intention of our money. If we allow our power and comfort to stand in the way of caring for every person of the world through our support of policy, or our lack of interest in social justice then we are no better than the rich man or the Pharisees. Our lives are an abomination.

We need the scripture, we need the prophet, we need Jesus to tell us, "You are the one."

Otherwise, we think we are doing the right thing. We give 10%, attend lunches in our honor for our giving, and pat ourselves on the back. What would happen if we gave 20%? Or 30%? Or downsized the house? Or gave away a car to a young family? What would happen if, instead of building trust funds for our children, we warned them that they would have to find their own path?

Bill and Melinda Gates, two of the richest people in the world, will leave nothing but an education stipend for their children. Their kids get nothing. No part of the estate. No portion of the stocks. No seat on the board. They did this so that their kids didn't get lazy. In a TED talk, Bill Gates said, "We want to strike a balance where they have the freedom to do anything but not a lot of money showered on them so they could go out and do nothing," Everything else will be given to charities. This is from a man who operates a foundation that has a 50 *billion* dollar *endowment*.

Following the prophet Nathan and Jesus Christ is an act of following radical life altering practices. Practices that shape how our spiritual DNA expresses itself in the ultimate epigenetic exercise. We have a choice to make, just like we do when choosing to drink too much, or smoke during pregnancy, or raise our kids in an anxious and angry household. We are shaping the kind of legacy we are leaving to the next generation. We must choose before the great chasm separates us from our ability to influence the world for God's Kingdom.

If we can do that, if we can make those hard choices, then the world we leave behind will truly be one of Good News, and we will alter the structure of everyone that comes after us forever. That is the power of a message and a practice that changes the building blocks of who we are.

13
What we leave Behind

Written as we celebrated homecoming with a congregation in North Carolina

EXODUS 33:12-23
MATTHEW 22: 34-46

There is a poem, which I think speaks to the story of the Hebrew slaves as they left Egypt, which I think sets the tone for us to talk a little more about Moses this morning. Here are a few lines from it:

> You may write me down in history
> With your bitter, twisted lies,
> You may tread me in the very dirt
> But still, like dust, I'll rise.
>
> Does my haughtiness offend you?
> Don't you take it awful hard
> 'Cause I laugh like I've got gold mines
> Diggin' in my own back yard.
>
> You may shoot me with your words,
> You may cut me with your eyes,
> You may kill me with your hatefulness,
> But still, like air, I'll rise.
> Out of the huts of history's shame, I rise
> Up from a past that's rooted in pain, I rise
> I'm a black ocean, leaping and wide,
> Welling and swelling I bear in the tide.
> Leaving behind nights of terror and fear, I rise
>
> Into a daybreak that's wondrously clear I rise
>
> Bringing the gifts that my ancestors gave,
> I am the dream and the hope of the slave.
> I rise
> I rise
> I rise.

Think of the slaves in Egypt. Think of the slaves in America. Think of immigrants and the poor reciting this poem. Think of ourselves possibly, as we too have experienced the shot of words and cutting eyes.

It's written by Maya Angelou, who in addition to writing seven autobiographies and other books and plays, was one of the most prolific and powerful poets that this country has ever seen. And yet, in the midst of all her work, she is also famous for saying this, "I have written eleven books, but each time I think, 'Uh oh, they're going to find out now. I've run a game on everybody, and they're going to find me out.'" Because oddly enough, Maya Angelou, this household name, this poet and author of renown, this voice in the wilderness suffered from something that we call now "imposter syndrome." Lots of people suffer with it, and it becomes a controlling factor in their lives that tells them over and over no matter what they achieve that they are, in fact, a fraud. And, as Mrs Angelou says, you keep thinking you are one book or one deal away from being found out. It's the feeling that we have that we really aren't; as smart or as good or as apt as people believe we are. It's that gnawing feeling that we can't really do whatever it is we have next to do in life, and even if we were to achieve it, then we simply cry our luck.

It's also one of the flaws that Moses possesses.

We might like to think of Moses as the conquering hero in this story of Exodus - winning this freedom he brought to the slaves of Israel. The truth of it is that Moses is a handsome man who is riddled with other issues. We can blame upbringing or social influence, but the fact is that Moses has deep anger issues, is a complete coward, and has blind fits in which he loses control. That's not to mention his lack of leadership skills, and his inability to speak in public. Add to that Moses' deep insecurity and never-ending feeling of being a man without a real home. It's a deeply tragic story.

Moses was taken in by the Pharaoh's daughter, who knew he was a Hebrew baby, but according to their own temple rituals, a gift from the Nile River gods could not be refused. So they are in a way forced to keep him. History tells us that they did, in fact, have another son who took the throne later, so this interloper, named for the act of a pagan god giving him up into the arms of the palace, had to live there with him. The Bible glosses over his youth and education as an Egyptian, because he was after all taken into the household of Pharaoh and practised alongside them all of their social ritual and educational system. But, scripture does come to one story that it thinks is important: Moses' connection with his own people.

He's grown up knowing that he was a Hebrew and that his people were slaves. So on this particular day, he ventures out to see them, and he witnesses their abuse. Because of the anger that he has pushed down inside him, he *chooses* to kill this Egyptian overseer -- the Bible says that Moses looked around to see if the coast was clear! Once he thought it was, he beat the man to death -- which is no quick feat. It is a long and firey process of strength and will and hate. Moses then disposes of the evidence and only runs away after he realizes that someone saw him, and Pharaoh found out about it and finally had the excuse he needed to kill Moses -- the one that got away from his original edict. It's a tale of Shakepsearian proportions, taken right out of the pages of MacBeth.

Moses heads into the desert and marries and has a child, and this is perhaps the saddest moment of all: his first born, the one that traditionally carries the name and the legacy of the father is named; Gershom. Which means foreigner. Not because Moses is currently a foreigner now, but because as Moses says, I was a foreigner, an immigrant, living in another country. Meaning Egypt. The legacy that Moses gives to his son is the long sad tale of someone who never felt like they belonged; who was outside every family group, both his actual race and the people that raised him. A feeling of never having a place.

This is the person God chooses to make a new family.

That is the heartbreaking power of the Almighty. To take someone so desperate, so filled with hate, and anger, and pain, and the desire to destroy things and to make them instead the creator of a new family. The leader of a group to which Moses and all of us could belong.

Because this story that we read, the story of Moses seeing the backside of God, is a story about that person -- who was still wrapped up in his own anger; who smashed the rock for water when people were complaining; who destroyed the law written on the tablets when he saw how weak some of his new family members were; who killed them for worshiping the calf; and who, because of his anger would never see the promised land. This man standing on the mountain with God Almighty, an honor afforded to no one else, needs *more*. More assurance that Moses isn't just some imposter. That there really isn't just some mistake that God chose him to do this work. Show me more Lord. Show me your face. Moses *knew* that would kill him.

Moses, twisted up in his own addiction to the power of the Almighty, was ready to die. God has more plans yet for him and hearing the need in his voice says, "Ok, but you can only see as much as will not kill you. Because... I know your name, Moses. I am with you."

Like a child climbing higher in a tree, or someone leaving for college or walking across the stage for the first time; Moses desperately needed to hear his only real parent, the only real parent he ever had in his life say those words: "I know your name. I am with you." Not the name that some Egyptian gave you Moses, your real name. The name of your spirit. The Hebrew here puts such emphasis on the word "name," and in the wake of knowing the name of God, "I am that I am," which Moses says he knows there is a parallel there that is immensely significant.

God says that he knows Moses, more intimately than anyone else on earth; "I am joyful over you. I am proud of you. I am, God is, pleased with you."

We all have our own legacy to leave behind. That's what a homecoming celebrates, isn't it? The legacy of this church that has stretched out far and wide across various geographies and families over the many years that it has been here. It's a time for the church to reel and say, "Wow" look at the reach, the impact, the hugeness of this family that we have continued to create in the name of Jesus Christ, this great family of God that is returning here also to hear some of those same words; "I know your name."

No matter where we have been or where we have gone, no matter if we have existed out in the world, feeling like a fraud or a success, you can always come home, and be known. That sentiment of being known is meaningful in this world. In a world where we have to sometimes take on a slightly different persona to succeed, in a world where we don't know how to attribute our successes, or in places where we feel like a failure. In places where we are berated and as Maya Angelou says "shot (with) words, cut with eyes, killed with hatefulness." It's good, so good, to have a place to call home where your family knows your name. The truth of you. The real you. To have those who promise to go with you after you leave. To walk the roads you have ahead, to send their presence, the presence of this church family with those that return back out into the world. That is precious.

Jesus had the opposite problem of Moses. Instead it was a whole lot of other people who thought Jesus was a fraud. There were six thousand Pharisees in the ancient world, and it seemed that all of them took a crack at Jesus in trying to prove that he was a fake. The Pharisees are often cast as a group of grumbling church leaders and mustache twisting villains, but their position in the ancient world was vastly more than that. During the time of Christ, the Hebrew children had no other types of leaders save those who were religious. Even the Roman authority, with the worship of the emperor, were religious authorities in their own right. So, in a very real way, the religious leaders were also the political authority of their day. The Sadducees were the highest social order as well as the highest level of Hebrew power in the land. The fact that Matthew states that the Sadducees had been silenced by Christ is no small thing. The Pharisees, gathered here in our reading, are in fact spurred on to action, because surely no upstart Galilean preacher is going to cowl the most powerful group of people in the country. The Pharisees ask him questions, seeking to tear Jesus down publicly in a show of their support of the rich and powerful authority.

Jesus' answer is, as many of us may know, an abbreviation for the ten commandments, which are themselves meant as a summary of the 600 plus codified laws that were the core of Hebrew beliefs. The first four commandments are ordered with respect to how creation should interact with the Almighty God, and the last six are a definition of how humanity should interact with itself as a creation of God. By answering, Jesus brings to bear an irrefutable response that says, "Not only are *all* of God's commandments the most important," by way of using this abbreviated illustration, "but also that the law itself given by God is simple and easy to follow and comes from a place of deep and abiding love."

The Pharisees are not caricatured villains. But they are deeply wrong, and like so many of us, when we are wrong, it usually comes from a place of desire for good things. Very seldom do people act foolishly or with cruelty because they are bad or eager to hurt one another. We all think that we are doing the right thing. The thing that proves our zeal for God, or for goodness or for our families or the thing that finally secures us as more than a fraud. The Pharisees started out on their journey just like Moses and just like all of us. Flawed people who had an encounter with God, who desperately wanted proof that they were known. Who wanted to see the face of God even if it killed them. But like Moses we let our emotions get the better of us, and like these religious leaders on the streets of Jerusalem, we fail to see the Messiah sitting in our laps.

It's much easier to codify our belief into neat little boxes that become a series of programmable If/then statements that we can follow. That's how the Hebrew people came to know their 600 and some rules of religion and purity. The book said that if you want to be close to God, follow this short 600 step plan! We want the security of knowing that what we are doing is right and good and we want to feel good about ourselves despite being made to feel like a fraud or a failure in our lives by social pressure or people who are meant to be our friends, or the success of others that becomes our measuring stick.

Like Moses, we become in that state, children without a real name yearning for a real home, who are sitting with God on the mountaintop but still begging for more. Begging for a promise, for assurance, for the cloak of Godliness which will show the world that we are God's people. We yearn for it, like Moses, in such a way that we will do anything to achieve that notoriety, that outward facing appearance so that the world will know at a glance that we are God's chosen people. And so many times like the Pharisees, all of our attempts at this on our own, make us false and ugly caricatures of ourselves, perceived as villains in the story.

Jesus says that love, simple love, is the answer. The love of God that hears Moses' request and ours and says, yes, I love you, I hear you, I choose you. If you love me with all that you are then I am pleased with you. If you love yourself, if you love your neighbor, the one you think hates you, then I know your name. And my presence will go with you.

Jesus says that every other part of the Law, and every word of the Prophets hangs on this concept. Everything. Jesus literally says that the whole rest of the accumulated knowledge of GOD, the whole story up to that moment was suspended by this understanding of Love of God, of ourselves and of others. That's it. Here's the answer you have been looking for Jesus says. Here is how you rise. Here is how you leave behind the nights of terror and fear. Here is how you leap like an ocean and put away the past rooted in pain. Here is how you rise.

When Jesus says that everything else we know about God, every other rule we want to come up with, every other dictate on how to act and live and be, when Jesus says that all of that hangs on this idea of love, it's a particular choice of words. They are in the same Greek words that were used in that time in regard to things suspended on a cross. This is the Son of God, speaking the Word of God, saying to these people and to us, "I hear you. If you want to know and be a part of this, if you have any doubt about what kind of love this is, then I will show you. I will show you the suffering, aching, totally sacrificial love that I mean. I will show you the love upon which your name resides. I will show you the Love that everything hangs on."

Jesus says to the Pharisees and Sadducees that it's not the love of rules or your thoughts on what is right and lawful. It's not the love of your social standing and power and wealth and authority. Not Moses, not the pain and torment and self inflicted doubt that you are trapped by. Not the hurt that you have in trauma and separation. But instead, the greatest commandment I can give you.

To fall into that love, to stand at the foot of the cross as someone who heard Jesus speak those words, surely *that* was a homecoming. That's the legacy we are charged to leave behind us, as a church and a people. That deep relaxation of the spirit, when we walk across that threshold of a place we call home, and realize that deep and abiding love that hangs there. In that precious and meaningful moment, regardless of our false names, or the social values that try to alter us, our true name is heard.

It is then that we rise.

14
In the Belly

Written after Malala Yousafzai published her second book, "We Are Displaced"

JONAH 2

I'm excited to be able to talk about one of only seven verses in scripture that mentions vomit.

In many ways, the book of Jonah should be strange to us. It has an endlessly reluctant prophet who is consumed by a large fish in a way that befuddles the scientific mind; Jonah is a man who wants destruction and balks at the Lord's good favor. It has no mention of Israel, as does every other prophet, and the only prophecy it has concerns a heathen city. Yet, we teach it to our children, unlike Micah or Nahum, and have them cut out pictures, wrongly, of whales.

We find ourselves here in this chapter of Jonah -- in the messiness. The messiness of the fish puke on the beach and that of Jonah's state of mind after his rebellion and aquatic consumption.

The book of Jonah continues with its strangeness by bringing us poetry in the midst of prose, a song in chapter 2. The Jewish cantor tradition preserves it: *Va-yo-mer ka-ra-tee mi'tza-ra-lee el-hashem:* "In my distress, I called to the Lord!" Have I missed something? Jonah is trapped. Is he singing here? Now? The other songs of scripture that are threaded into the prose seem like they belong. The song of Moses, the song of Deborah, are victory hymns. Hannah's song of praise, Hezekiah who sings upon the event of his recovery.

And Jonah. Who sings from the belly of a fish.

We find ourselves here with Jonah, crying out in this poetry to God from a place that should have no song. A place that should have no hope. A place of utter darkness, a place from which there is no possible escape. Jonah admits in these verses that this is the place of the dead --that he is deep in that realm. Jonah, the prophet has been banished. This is a place that reeks, a place that clogs up our senses, eyes watering, throat gagging. The footing isn't solid, the undulation of the giant fish can be felt continuously. The sounds of gastric events overcome every other noise. The belly of this creature is like *Sheol*. This is a place that is designed for digestion, not prayer.

In thinking of turmoil I am reminded of a girl. She has been in and out of the news since 2009. Her name is Malala Yousafzai. She is from Pakistan and lives in a district named for the Swat river in the northern part of that country. In 2009 the Taliban ruled her village and banned girls from attending school. She was 12. She began writing an online blog under a false name detailing her life under the extremists' rule. It's an incredible story, and when reading her blogs, it would be easy to see her situation as a time without hope, a place that emulated Jonah's story. Her name literally means "grief stricken." Surely as a young girl under Taliban rule this was the lowest point of her dark period, and through it she continued speaking out for the importance of education for women. The Pakistani military liberated the region. Girls returned to school, and all seemed well. In October of 2012, Malala survived an assassination attempt. She survived a gun-shot to head and neck that took place as she was returning home from school. On the bus. Local Islamic mosques condemned the Taliban publicly but the Taliban still said that they intended to kill this girl and her father. This year she turned 19. She's published a book and appeared on the cover of Time this past April. She is the youngest person ever to have been nominated for a Nobel Peace prize. She was even on the Daily Show with Jon Stewart. She has of course been asked what her response was to the hatred that the Taliban have for her and her family. To this she replies *that in response to evil you must not treat others with cruelty, but when you fight them you must fight them with peace, and dialogue and education [Paraphrased]*. She does admit that her initial response was to hit them with her shoe.

    Here is a girl who is faced with the very real threat of death, and refuses to compromise her heart. When it would be so much easier, even now, to recant, to slip away silently for the sake of her own life, or for her father's, still, she is ever hopeful and presses on. When I hear stories like that and I consider my own hopeless moments, I feel like a fraud. But it might be that I am in good company.

    Jonah's song as we read this morning is a recount of lines from the Psalms and Deutornomy. Well known by Jonah, nearly every line from verse 2 to verse 9 is a reference[18]. Jonah is comparing his plight to the saints of old. When Jonah says that he has been cast out of the sight of God, he means it fairly. It's an acceptance, and an understanding that it is what Jonahs deserves because of his own flight from God. For Jonah his sin has become his punishment. As in verse 9, Jonah emulates his forefathers in making a thanksgiving sacrifice of his belief in anticipation of sure deliverance. At the end of this song from this place, Jonah feels assured of his deliverance.

    And we might applaud Jonah's amazing ability to grasp hope in the midst of a hopeless situation. It seems like the kind of solid belief that we can expect from the great prophets... but I don't think that's it. I think Jonah is a fraud, just like me.

    He is a prophet who ran from the first real call he had! He abjectly disobeyed God in a command to bring to peace and blessing and real life to

---

[18] Psalm 130, Deuteronomy 30:4, Psalm 30:3

a whole city of people. And he refuses because of his own prejudice. Even his prayer in the darkest hour *seems* like one that is full of all the right things. I think God brought him up out of that great fish, not because he had finally learned his lesson, but because God had more to teach him. God isn't honoring the confidence he is showing in his prayer, but bringing him out of one place to give Jonah another chance at real understanding.

Consider the prayer; aside from the whole thing being selfish and filled with I statements (and not one mention of the poor sailors who might still be in danger of shipwreck, as far as Jonah knows). Verse 8 has Jonah condemning the idolaters -- knowing that is who God is sending him to save. He puts himself in contrast "But I," Jonah promises that he *will do* these things, sacrifice to God, give shouts of grateful praise, but it's conditional. And it is something that the idolaters of the ship he was just on have already done days ago. This prayer sounds more like a masked complaint.

Jonah doesn't get it. The men on the boat have a conversion after throwing Jonah in -- God knows that Jonah needs to see that, to witness the redemption that can take place. To do this, God puts Jonah in the worst place imaginable. In all other uses of the word for vomit in scripture the connotation is -- expectedly--negative. Jonah will re-enter his ministry lower than anything else on the beach and certainly lower than anything else in the town. His luggage? Still on the boat, or perhaps it was thrown off before they tossed him in. His clothes? Well, they have a great and pleasant odor.

When we read it like this, maybe it seems like this bright spot in the belly of the fish doesn't really happen, and perhaps the candle of hope in the dark isn't there. If Jonah is just a fraud like me, complaining about basically nothing in the face of real world and local tragedy, then where is the good news in this passage?!

The hope in hopelessness falls on the last line, not of the prayer, but of the chapter. Not verse 9, but verse 10.

"And the Lord commanded the fish."

It takes place in God commanding the fish. Hope takes place in the actions of God. Because in this we see a God who is not content to let someone, who can't see the Grace of God, stay in darkness. This Grace that is going to be prepared for a faithless people - that's something that God *has* to show to his prophet.

Because real *hope* in these terrible times is tied to *grace*. Hope is tough when it's tied to grace and forgiveness, but it has to be. If we allow our notion of hope to be tied to past action, to history, to everything we know, to events - then those things are going to lead us to despair, or at the very least, to an entitled sense of hubris like Jonah. "I know God will save me because of my heritage as a chosen prophet. I know God will save me because the Psalmist, and Moses say so. I know that I am not like those heathen idolaters." If you read the first chapter of Jonah, you are asked to look beyond your Tarshish and instead to the uncomfortable places. Here Jonah sits in the most uncomfortable place imaginable, and he *still* can't see Nineveh, the place he is supposed to be. Not really. Not how God sees it: as a place and a people loved and worthy of redemption.

We have places of utter darkness, places that we feel have no possible escape. Places that feel like the place of the dead. We can feel that we have been banished. We can be in situations that clog up our senses, that make our eyes water, and places which have no stable footing. Places that do not seem designed for prayer or for hope.

Yet from those places, we have to know that God can command anything in our lives, including us. God has a will that we not be kept in that place. It's not our own actions or the recognition of our own inherent goodness that get us out, but simply who God is. God is a God who places his Son at the cross. A God of forgiveness and love for even a city of idolaters. Our hope comes with the actions of this God. It comes with the forgiveness we receive and in our forgiveness of others. Not just other people, but forgiveness of other histories, whole modes of thinking, entire paradigms. It comes with the forgiveness of things that we thought we knew about others, or even things we thought we knew about ourselves. There is true hope. Not hope like Jonah can give, but hope like only the Lord can supply. This is the hope that drove Paul to write to the Colossians. A hope that the church there could thrive in forgiveness to a new place that didn't rely on what they knew, or remembered about the past. A people that performed the Gospel of Christ in word and deed. The kind of thing that leads to thanksgiving.

That is the only answer to a truly hopeful life.

Thanksgiving.

The truest testimony *against* Jonah, as we will come to find out, is his total lack of thanksgiving. The sacrifice that Jonah promised, that never came, is the thankful shout of grateful praise. The giving that we do, of ourselves, or of our gifts and offerings, is not tied to duty or a contractual understanding of support, but out of this new hope that dwells in our lives through Jesus Christ. We dwelt in the place of death; we were there, and sometimes still visit frequently, but the truth is that the beach is waiting.

The God who gives Jonah hope, is the one who gives hope to us and to the world in the form of a Savior. As hopeful people brought out of darkness, we meet the world with grace and forgiveness. We live and worship in joy and gratitude, not because there is no darkness, but because we can be a witness to power that will always overcome it.

15
All Things

JOB 38:4-21
COLOSSIANS 1:15-20

Every year there are multiple opportunities to celebrate God's incredible creation. Earth day, several conservation days, National Parks day. Ulessys S Grant, president when the first National Park Yellowstone was created, long thought that land given over to the public trust would be a "respite for the soul." So, in talking about creation we begin, not with the first creation stories from Genesis but instead with these words from Job and Colossians. Here we will see that the elements of creation and the connection between God, creation, and the beloved children are tightly woven throughout scripture.

In our passage from Colossians, we have Paul showing us clearly the supremacy of the Son of God which pertains to some specific things going on at the church in eastern Turkey, and as we are looking at Creation, we see that Paul says that Christ, the image of God, is tied to all creation. This isn't totally new information. It could be a reminder of some of what the Gospel of John has to say as the Word being present with God in the very beginning. Paul moves ahead and creates one of his most profound descriptions of who Christ *is* over the natural creation found in all that exists as well as being first in the spiritual creation of the church itself.

Creation, Paul says, is made through Christ.

We benefit then from checking the characteristics that Paul lists when describing Christ. There is a sense of wonder and adoration worship, and as Paul does in many places, his writing is not just rhetoric but worship, not just theology but is relationally tying God and humans together. There is still more to see about Christ, so there is more to dissect in this passage that has lent itself to creation.

Paul describes Jesus Christ as a Reconciler;

"For God was pleased to have all his fullness dwell in him, and through him to reconcile to himself all things..."[19] Whatever rifts or divisions that exist between any parts of Creation, Christ is the means and the path by which those rifts will be healed. Between people, between humanity and mutually beneficial existence with the natural world - everything that exists finds reconciliation in Christ.

Paul describes Jesus as Peaceful.

---

[19] Colossians 1:19-20

In Paul's understanding, Christ makes peace through his blood, shed on the cross. Not simple peace as the absence of conflict, but the wholeness found conceptually in the Jewish Shalom. The perfectness, the peace that can only be found in a thing expressing perfectly it's created intent by God.

Jesus is *Creator*.

At several places in scripture, Christ is revealed as creator of all things[20]. Seen and unseen, the two forms that make up the universe in its totality. Jesus is there at the founding of it all

Paul tells us that Jesus Christ is the *Indwelt of God, Supreme.*

For Christ to be anything less is, as one Anglican bishop and author from the turn of the century put it, "a bridge broken at the farther end."[21] Jesus must be this, or the salvation of Christ is without foundation. The saving power of Grace in Christ must also be, as Jesus says, "I am in the Father and the Father in me," from John 14.

Do we struggle with God expressed through Christ as Reconciler? Peacemaker? Creator? Or Supreme? At what places do these roles start to make us uncomfortable? When God desires to reconcile our enemies? When real reconciliation asks us to look deeply inward at places in our own uncomfortable life events? When the peace of the world forces us to make real and unpopular choices? When the lack of peace in our own lives leads us to focus on our anger issues?

What about as a Creator? When God, when the Sovereign of Love and Jesus our Savior are at the heart of *all things* created, does it give us pause when we analyze our consumptive nature? Are we in awe and respect of God's creation, or do we act as the un-creators in the world laying waste to what God has made? At what point do these roles force us to get uncomfortable? When does the supremacy of Christ in all things cause us to reconsider our feelings of being right? When do we rail at God and say that *we* know best?

Job, which is the oldest book in the Bible and possibly the world, is a story that deals with the oldest and most human of problems. Isn't that fantastic? The first story that God's people wanted to write down is the one about this very human frailty. The accounting of the way we feel when our lives are hard and full of pain.

Job is the epicenter of what inevitably goes wrong with all human beings at one time or another. We become obsessed with ourselves in the midst of our success. We can pay lip service as it is implied that Job does, and we say the words that attribute our vaunted success to God's favor on us knowing deep down that we deserve it because we are smart or special or hardworking or good looking.

---

[20] John 1:1-4, John 17:5, Hebrews 1:1-2
[21] Anglican Bishop H.C.G. Moule, 1841-1920

It is only in Job's *tragedy* that the real theology comes through. Likewise, it is only in our brokenness that we have the chance to see what kind of believer we are. Job's friends say that his tragedy came because of something he must have done, that God only punishes bad people. If you look around you today, we know that's not true. Bad people often have power and what looks like blessings and prosperity. In the midst of all this bad counsel from his friends, Job cracks and finally demands that an unjust God answer him.

Are you in pain? Are you right now wondering if God is there, if the cosmic order of the universe has it out for you and the total loss of your life has brought all things crashing down around you?

You are in good company. There is a painting that I would love to see in person that depicts Job. It is by Léon Bonnat[22] a 19th-century french painter known for portraits. It shows Job in full figure, in the midst of pain crying out silently to God.

God's response is not as comforting as we might expect. God's response is a challenge, with a poetic show of what all things are.

God's response is an invitation in the form of a question; Were you there when I made you? Can you view the world as the expression that God has for what God has made?

This is why an awe of creation is important. And why the destruction of creation, the carelessness with which we can approach it, is dangerously callous, and against God.

We desperately need to cry out from our loneliness and pain and be met with wonder.

With the wonder of creation in stars and the gravitational eddies that surround them, with wonder at the way good music of any kind can speak to us deeply. We must see with wonder the way things grow, and lie dormant, and the way that strangers and our church family can surprise us with their love.

If we do not, we will never understand God or Christ, since Paul tells us that the image of God in Christ is present, and the vessel through which this was all created.

That Peace, that Care, that Sovereignty, the Reconciliation -- this is the way through which all things came into being. Job, after the speech that God has for him, is able to see. Is able to wonder and marvel at the universe. At the painstaking beauty of it, at the Love that went into each particle. So must we too be able to see the wonder, to be practised in it.

If we do not, we will turn inward for our answers and consume ourselves in the process.

Our theologies will become toxic and poisonous, and quickly forget the Truth of our God who made all things.

---

[22] Léon Joseph Florentin Bonnat, 1833 - 1922 (aged 89)

Paul writes from prison, and Job cries out from the prison of his situation.

In both cases there is a choice. Paul could look inward at his own strength and clout as a Roman citizen. He could lash out at God for his circumstance. He could bemoan the political power of the Roman authority over him and its obstruction of his message. Or he could tell others about the perfect power over all things that is held in Jesus Christ.

Job does rail at heaven in his situation. Job goes down a bad path, looking to his own wisdom and that of his friends and family. There is the demand that God infuse him with new wisdom, as his previous understanding of the world and his place in it has failed him utterly. The way God sets Job back on the path is to list out the many creations across the span of the universe. It is then, upon being brought to consider creation, that Job finally and fully sees, and then repents.

For a long time in Job, the guy sticks to his guns and says he has nothing to repent for, going so far as to list out all the rules and ideals by which he lives his life... yet after his revelatory moment of true seeing... He repents in dust and ashes.

Job's real sinful nature, as revealed by his trial of circumstance, was not being able to see God in all things. Job only saw God in his blessings. His wealth, his family, his position socially (remember these are ancient problems, but they seem all too familiar to us). Once the God of *all things* was revealed, Job began to see God everywhere.

This is why creation is important.

This is why we need to study more deeply our connection to the created world. Not because Jesus was some tree-hugging hippie with big plans for us if we could only save the dolphins, but because we ignore the Essence of God in *All Things* at our peril, theologically and spiritually. It goes way beyond recycling.

The concept of "all things" as it appears here in Colossians is a Greek word that is both simple and complex at the same time. *Pas*, not to be confused with the Latin *pax*, is a word that *does* mean "all" but it really should read "all the all." It means everything that is before and afterwards. If I said "all the people of the city," using this Greek word to the ancient world, an image would come to mind of every group in the city, at every age, and those whose feet were even just now walking across the border of the city and joining its population. It is both the whole and the individual pieces counted together; the large and small picture at once, the beach and every grain of sand, the forest and each tree. It is truly *all* of the things.

All things are Reconciled, All things are made Peaceful and whole, All things have been Created, and over all things is Christ Supreme.

These words in Colossians were not a call for people to write letters to the Roman senators about the issues most pressing to all decent Christians.

This is a statement about the radical order of the universe. The unalterable, undeniable state in which the present continuity of existence resides without the possibility of change.

If we are in prison, if we are in pain, we have choices to make. If we are coasting on our laurels and enjoying a theology shaped by a happy family and healthy wealth, we still have the same choices to make.

How will we experience the image of God? The all that Christ *is*, as expressed by everything.

Paul writes from prison to the church in Colossae because they are making choices about how to move forward as Christians. They were starting to favor a law code, mandatory circumcision, asceticism, angel worship and some other things. They were looking inward. They stood in their own personal pain like Job and *demanded* order and outlines from God. Paul's response was to recenter them on Christ with the same illumination that is found in Job. Christ, as the indwelt incarnate God, orders the morning and knows where the light and the darkness reside. Seek *all things*, and you will find Christ bearing the image of the Almighty.

This is what will bring us the truth and our own repentance.

Because who can look at "all things" and not give in to Job's admission of knowing nothing and retiring to the ashpit?

For years, I have occasionally enjoyed reading through the populist publications of a lot of astrophysicists. Everything from Einstein and Hawking to Goldsmith and Nakajima. It seemed like a natural leap for me to go from a love of "Star Trek" and "Dr. Who" to reading about quantum particle behaviors, string theory and galactic nurseries where stars are formed. As you read through a lot of that stuff all at once, you get to a point where your eyes slowly close, and you start having a tough time wrapping your head around contemplating the spaces between subatomic particles and the way that speed affects the passage of time as affected by gravity and the possible intergalactic presence of dark matter. It's a little scary. The vastness of it all is intimidating.

Just how in the world are we supposed to truly consider God in all things? After reading through the poetry of Job, or really just having an experience with creation, how can we consider the gates of death and the fathoms of the ocean?

It comes to us, like many things, through a kind of training. A refocusing of our spiritual eye, like Job, who before had only heard but now had seen. We must take it all in bites, in doses, in capsules, so that we can digest it.

We have to keep engaging in the stories of Creation. We can see scripture and the first words of the Bible describe God's loving making of all things. We can consider how we are stewards of this created world. How water comes alive to us through Christ, and how our bread gives life. We can consider the birds of the air as well as seeing how the groaning and lament of creation is still very much with us today.

We, like the church at Colossae, are more fortunate than Job. We get to encourage one another, hear one another and help each other as we attempt to see the image of God in Christ through whom *all things* were made.

That is an important thing because there are of course other places where the authors use that Greek *pas* meaning all things, notably again from Paul in Corinthians. Maybe you have been thinking about it already as we have continued to repeat the refrain of all things; All things are bourne, all things are hoped for, all things are endured, all things are believed in by Love. Truly, we serve a God of all things, a God of Creation and Power and Reconciliation and Rulership, and yes, Love.

We are not left in prison, or in our pain, or in lament of our loss. Out of Love, out of the "all things" found in Love, we are invited and welcomed into a new way of seeing all creation that will change and reshape our lives.

16
Partnering with the Spirit

Written after millions of refugees fled Syria and were met in the US and Europe with fear

ACTS 8:26-40
ISAIAH 56:1-8

There are more refugees every day. In the last few years the number has risen by 2.9 million people to over 400 million people[23] today. People are displaced by war, by famine, or by oppressive and harmful regimes. The world has always had a movement of people seeking a new start. That's how this country got its start after all.

Opening with that stark number isn't a shock tactic. This scripture, both really, are specifically talking about refugees. The alien. The foreigner; in Hebrew the *nekar*, is literally "the stranger," and understood by Hebrew scholars to mean refugee. A person seeking a new start, fleeing from their old life. In fact, Dr Sigve Tonstad, a Bible professor from the University of St. Andrews, said that the refugee is the most extreme and perfect example of the "alien/other" in scripture.

The reading seems to be slanted to be *for* the refugees. Isaiah is, in part, speaking directly to them, calling on them to relax. "Don't worry," says God, "You are going to be accepted by my people." In verse 3, God is talking to a crowd who fully expect to be separated out, to be kept apart from the people of God and in a turn of the expectation, God says, "No, no, that's not how my people act." In fact, later in verses 6-8 God explains exactly what then can expect.

The refugees are encouraged to join themselves to the Lord, and to keep the Sabbath, which as we can recall is one of the guidelines that God set out for the people he loves. The order of the day here is that if you can love the name of God (who wouldn't after being welcomed in?), then the Blessing is yours.

Here, however, we have to go back and see again what the Sabbath command entailed. No work certainly, that was the surface rule, but the Sabbath brought with it a host of other instructions that parse out just exactly what it really means. If we read the instructions carefully from Deuteronomy 5,[24] we can see that there is indeed a special slant on the Sabbath that favors the slave, immigrant, or stranger. It does this specifically because God

---

[23] UNHCR numbers reported in 2019
[24] Deuteronomy 5:12-15

reminds his children that we were *all* exiles at one time. It's written then, into this code of law.

This form of equity might not have existed anywhere else in the ancient world, except on the Sabbath, God's Holy day. It was unique and special, and meant to be protected. Our own Walter Brueggemann had a great quote about the dangers of not observing the Sabbath principles, saying that, "Landed people are tempted to create a Sabbath-less society in which land is never rested, debts are never canceled, slaves are never released; nothing is changed from the way it now is and has always been."

So the invitation to keep the Sabbath for the refugee is a promise of equality to those seeking refuge, and a reminder of the Deuteronomic Law set down by God as the children of God were themselves fleeing slavery and death. I hope we can see that this isn't an "if/then" statement being created here in Isaiah. Or at the very least, not only an "if/then." God isn't holding the adherence to the Sabbath over the heads of the refugees like a carrot, but instead is insisting that *this* is the new way of life among the people of God. Rest and equity.

But then God goes one step further.

God *brings* them to the Holy Mountain. The place where God first wrote the Law! The place where one can have an experience with the Almighty. God is going to make them *joyful;* these people who have come from another country, beaten, tired, and battered. Whatever they bring to worship with, however their sacrifices come, they will be accepted.

Because, God says, the House of Prayer is for all people.

Wow.

That's an amazing and powerful message to people who are fleeing their homes, or starving in their own countries. For people who have been threatened with war and death, the promise of life and joy and rest and acceptance must sound like the trickling of pure water to thirsty people.

The Hebrew word for prayer that is used here, *tephilah*, sounds pretty lyrical and is also used to mean a "hymn." So the weary are joyfully welcomed into a place of song.

In the words of the Westminster Confession, what we have are these two groups of people "glorifying God and enjoying him forever."

That sounds like a Sabbath that any stranger could gladly keep .

We are the people of Israel in this message and God speaks to the refugee, the other, the stranger, and the eunuch on our behalf. Most likely we don't know what it is like to be the foreigner. There is a poem called "Home" by Warsan Shire, a Kenyan born poet, that was written in 2015, and she translates in it some of the things that we will never know about being that stranger:

"No one leaves home unless
home is the mouth of a shark.
You only run for the border
when you see the whole city running as well

your neighbors running faster than you
breath bloody in their throats
the boy you went to school with
who kissed you dizzy behind the old tin factory
is holding a gun bigger than his body
you only leave home
when home won't let you stay.

No one leaves home unless home chases you
fire under feet
hot blood in your belly
it's not something you ever thought of doing
until the blade burnt threats into
your neck
and even then you carried the anthem under
your breath
only tearing up your passport in an airport toilets
sobbing as each mouthful of paper
made it clear that you wouldn't be going back.
you have to understand,
that no one puts their children in a boat
unless the water is safer than the land
...
no one chooses refugee camps
or strip searches where your
body is left aching
or prison,
because prison is safer
than a city of fire"
...

    We can't write that poem. I certainly can't. I don't really know that story, and my grandparents, as many of you know, were from Syria and Lebanon. But God knew that story. When God spoke through the prophet Isaiah, when God said, I have a word for the people. For my people, for all people. God knows this poetry deeply and so greets the refugee, the unknown strangers, with song and Sabbath, and acceptance of their offerings. That's powerful.

Maybe we don't intimately know that story that drives people from "home," but we do know how powerful that word of God is, that acceptance, that song. We've experienced it here in this community.

We have had the privilege and honor of partnering with and loving an incredible refugee family from Afghanistan. You've heard us talk and write of "the Nooris" many times before, and this past week we saw their eldest son write a deeply thankful note to the people of this church. Not too long ago many of us met in the Fellowship Hall to have lunch with them and to tell them how much we've grown to care about them, and to love them as a part of our family. We heard him speak firsthand of their utterly unspeakable gratitude and love. We've offered them rest at the sacrifice of our work. God has brought them song, and acceptance and a joyful place on that Holy Mountain. That is incredible.

But it's not just refugees, or foreigners who feature in this passage, but eunuchs as well. They get the same treatment and promise, except for a seemingly wholly distasteful joke about not being "cut off" in verse 5, which I can only imagine was some poetic license taken by Isaiah. It's not just the English translation either, the Hebrew *karath* means "to cut," as in a body part. I mean, come on. In truth though, the Hebrew also has ties to the way that covenants were made by slicing meat to be shared between the covenanting parties. So, truly, the line is more about a person who has no family being then invited in and becoming part of a new family. Given a new name. A name that would go on and on for generations whether they had any children or not. Which to someone who has no family is, again, powerful.

Eunuchs feature in both of our verses this morning and that is for a very specific reason which we will see later. Yet in our account from Luke in Acts chapter 8, we have a very different kind of eunuch. Not escaping persecution, but instead riding in a carriage. In fact, well off enough to be reading a precious scroll of the book of Isaiah as he went, which I connect with. I love reading on long trips. In this scene is our first little line about the coming Good News moment with Philip. The passage tells us that his carriage is traveling from Jerusalem to Gaza. Now, for anyone who has ever traveled to Palestine, or looked on a map, you know that the Palestinian city of Gaza is actually to the west of Jerusalem. It's on the coast. But Ethiopia is far to the south and east... Where is the eunuch going? Luke is hinting at something, even though the Eunuch is a follower of Judaism, he's going the wrong way.

Having established that, I feel like we need to establish something else as well. What exactly is a eunuch? Now, I am going to hope and move ahead with the understanding that we all get the graphic details and instead turn to the Biblical accounts on this. The Bible uses the word eunuch in several different ways, and the root of the word is a help to us here. We actually get the English word from the Greek, *eunucos*. This word is two words brought together: *eunous*, meaning "good-minded," and *echein*, meaning "to have." This is a contraction of a Greek expression meaning "to be good in mind; to be loyal, good-natured." This understanding of the world sheds light on Jesus' comments in Matthew 19 about some people being "born as eunuchs." I don't want to spend too much time on this, but it is important to understand as we compare these verses and see what the eunuch represents in the ancient world.

It is a similar story in the Old Testament. Our verse from Isaiah 56 has the Hebrew, *sārēs*, while coming from a castration or cutting root, is also translated elsewhere in the Old Testament as simply "official." The idea that the eunuch was simply a guard for the concubines is a total misinterpretation of this, and comes out of much later sources that looked to things like the *Harem Ağası*, from the Ottoman Empire's tradition, who truly were "Haram Watchers." In the Old Testament, Pharaoh's butler and his baker from the story of Joseph were also called *sārēs* yet are translated as to simply be part of Pharaoh's court.

So the eunuch then in the Old and New Testament, is simply someone who is a government employee. A trusted person. And while there were definitely connotations, as part of that position, or as Jesus says in Matthew, their own inclinations, they had no children or families, the physical limitations of that varied. The point is not their physically imposed or chosen lifestyle however, but instead their role as people of government.

It's meaningful for God to be reaching out to them.

The government for a persecuted people means something very different than it does to you or me. To ones who had fled Egypt, and been under the thumb of the Babylonians, the Assyrians, and the Romans, governments are usually the bad guys in the story.

Luke's writing in Acts in the ancient days might have perked up a few ears as they listened. "An official from another empire?" they would ask. Great. Yet, this man is a believer. A God-fearer, someone who was allowed a place in the faith because of that very passage from Isaiah (and it's no mistake that he's reading from that book). This is someone who would have been seen as a total outsider and because of his role in government, doubly suspicious and suspect. And yet... The spirit of the Lord had other plans.

You will note that in this verse from Acts, it's not Philip who gets an idea. It's not Phillip who goes over to the carriage of his own accord. The spirit tells him to do something in both instances. The spirit tells Phillip to hit the road. The Spirit then again tells Philip to go to the carriage and join it. So he jogs over and hears the eunuch reading. To what end is this encounter? Good News. A revelation. A life totally altered, something of the Gospel taken back to the far off country of Ethiopia - you will notice that the verse says he went on his way. Not to Gaza though, because now he's on the right path.

It was our ancient Biblical lesson from Isaiah that brought him there. The prophet laid the groundwork for that person and probably millions like him to become part of the family of God. This verse in Isaiah was the foundation for Phillip having the chance to bring the Good News, the Gospel of Jesus Christ into his life. Just imagine, if the eunuch hadn't been allowed in the country to worship in Jerusalem. The story could have ended with a whimper as he was turned away for who he was, and instead ends with a soul inflamed by the Holy Spirit.

Make no mistake, the Spirit is present in the Old Testament; it's there witnessing to this passage in Isaiah, encouraging the people of God to hear it and to act accordingly. The spirit partnered with the children then to see themselves in the eyes and face of the unknown stranger, and in the government official from another land who had no family.

Phillip partnered with the spirit by hearing the word of God through the angel. The messenger sent him an order and gave a command. He didn't discuss the validity of the foreigners' place in God's kingdom because he knew his Bible and already knew how God felt about both foreign people and eunuchs working for the government. He found himself in a place of service.

This is what we are bad at. What I am bad at. We don't hear the urging of God or take our scripture seriously enough to move and act on them. We infringe our own experiences on the call. We think about last time. We think about our feelings. We hear the voices of our friends.

We don't want to partner with the Spirit, not really. We want it to obey us and do as we see fit. We want the Spirit to fit into our worldview of rightness, and we want the power of God to be present in our choices. We aren't willing to be wrong. We aren't willing to hear the hard voice of the Word of God telling us that the eunuch and the unknown alien *already* have a place in God's Kingdom.

For some reason, for some wholly human and unGodly reason, our desire is to shut out the refugee. Even the word eunuch makes us cringe a little; the idea of strangers is not a comforting one.

God does not shut them out. These verses are not only a mandated instruction on how to partner with the Spirit, and how we should react to the stranger, the foreigner, the unknown government worker, and the family-less, but they are also how the stranger should feel about themselves. God not only hears their hearts but is speaking *to* them.

It's a moment of beauty really. God is speaking to *them* not to us. Not to the children already present. God is talking to them, saying, "Don't call yourselves unworthy. I make you worthy. Don't say that you have nothing to offer the world, I will create a place for you and I will lift you up and *honor* you."

Let me tell you that when the King of all Creation says that a place of Honor has been made for you -- the people who try to tear that down should be cautious.

We have problems partnering with the Spirit. We don't really want to, though sometimes we say we do, but the fact is we don't really have a choice. We have committed ourselves as God's people. The scene has been set. God has heard our pledge that we have made on the blood of Jesus Christ.

The angel is coming. So we'd better be watchful. We've done some amazing things, just like Phillip did earlier in Acts. We've been a blessing to this city and to our communities, but God isn't waiting around to let us rest on our laurels. God has that angel coming, and God is going to be knocking on our doors with the next mission, the harder thing. The thing that takes us right next to the eunuch, the foreigner, the stranger, the one that makes us the most uncomfortable or afraid. The one that God has already placed in the Kingdom, the one that is already honored, and interested in the Word of God. The one who is reading but might not get the whole picture. The moment is ripe and there will soon be a day when the messenger of the Almighty comes knocking on our door, ready to partner up and do the hard work of believing and acting like people of faith and trust and love.

If we are God's people, Sabbath people, partnering with the Spirit people, then we will be ready.

17
The Good Thing

Written for students who held me accountable for division in my own life

LUKE 10:25-37
LEVITICUS 9:9-1

In this reading from Luke, Jesus is starting to gain some notoriety. The seventy-odd disciples have been sent out and have been spreading his message and casting out demons, and we pick up the story from there.

Jesus is being put to the test. The question is put to Jesus from someone already proved in the law, someone who has been through the advanced study classes, and who has made a name for himself as an expert in matters of Mosaic tradition. Jesus knows immediately what the question is, not a seeking of information, but a test, a way of trying to catch this new rabbi in some blasphemy. His followers have been out in the countryside preaching and driving out demons. It's time to double check Christ's references and put the new guy through the paces.

Jesus' famous answer in the form of the parable is less a commentary on the relationship between the Jews and the Samaritans and more a description of the injustice that lies in the heart of the one asking the question.

It's a way for Christ to say, "You know the law, but you are not practicing it."

A while back I was working at a church that was in need of reconciliation. Their students, their adults - the whole church was reeling from the trauma of several events managed by their previous pastor. I wasn't going to judge, but I knew we needed to make some progress quickly in order to move on as a church family and heal together. For many months I went about the process of preparing myself mentally and spiritually to facilitate the healing process, especially in the youth group. We were having great movement with the students, and I was getting the impression that they were really taking hold of the ideas I was bringing out and allowing themselves to heal some of the rifts.

Then something unforeseen happened.

I was working with the students one night, and I felt like the group needed a story about the destructive force that grudge holding could have. To that end, I told them a personal story about a one-time friend of mine with whom I had a great falling out. It was just after college, and while we split the rental of a house, over several weeks my friend and I fought. We bickered back and forth, and the friendship finally imploded dramatically as I moved out, never to speak to each other again. There were many factors that played a part in it; ambiguous terms of our living conditions, differences in core needs from the home we shared, a high anxiety level as we were all starting our careers after college. It came to blows at one point and, seething, I counted that as the last straw.

In recounting this to the students, I felt like it was having the desired effect. I held their attention and I could tell they understood the terrible emotions that this grudge had in my life and in the lives of people around me. They could tell how hard it was for me to let it go, to be at peace, and to finally let all ill will toward my one time friend dissolve.

As I was about to launch into a connecting piece between my story and their own, a hand went up. One of the students asked me, "Did you guys ever become friends again?"

I paused.

In my eagerness to help these students move beyond their battle, it never occurred to me to remember that my own struggle wasn't truly over. Because the answer was- no! I hadn't talked to him again. We had never discussed what happened in the intervening decade. We had never made peace. So, I realized, like the elder of the Law in this reading, that I knew the law, but did not practice it.

It is interesting to try and gauge Jesus' mood in this interchange. I don't think he was perturbed fielding questions, I think he expected it, and – we sometimes forget – counted the elder of the Law as one of God's beloved children. Jesus loves this man who is asking him these questions. His intent then is not to maliciously tear him down or prove him foolish, but to alter him, to teach him, and to bring him back into righteousness. With that in mind I think Jesus' mood is good. Happy even, to have the chance to explore the issue.

The elder's understanding of neighbor came from Leviticus 19, in which it describes the other children of the tribes as "neighbor." Jesus takes it further into territory not mentioned in that Old Testament passage, but which gets to the power behind the Law that was written.

Usually we identify with one of two characters in the parable. Either the man on the road who is beaten, or the Samaritan. But I wonder if we have these characters right when we imagine this? The man on the road is left for dead. As the downtrodden, this person cannot act on his own behalf. He is totally dependent on others. The people that this beaten man would expect to help do not – because of their strict adherence to the law – and the hated enemy is instead the healer and the savior. The Samaritan goes above and beyond at every turn. When we picture ourselves as this man, do we imagine our rescue coming at the hands of our enemy?

On the other side of things, we imagine ourselves as the Samaritan, magnanimously lending a helping hand to someone in need. But it's not just anyone we are reaching out to. We are reaching out as the Samaritan to our *persecutor*. We are helping the very person who despises us. The agitator who hates and condemns us at every opportunity. That's who we are saving. That's who we are nursing back to health.

The verse in Leviticus from chapter 19 and surrounding are known as the laws of Justice and Mercy. When Christ asks about mercy in our New Testament passage, he is asking, "Who in this story followed the law?" And the elder of the Law has no choice but to answer "My enemy. The one I despise." Jesus says, "if the Samaritan is following the law, and following the love of God in loving his neighbor, the one you despise, who has the key to eternal life?"

That is an infinitely harder message to live out, and perhaps harder still for us to preach to the world. It seems easy in comparison to instead simply imagine that we are the powerful and better person, reaching down to lift up our fallen enemy with compassion. But that's not what is happening. Our enemy is lifting us up. Or, we are not reaching out to the one we hate, but we are reaching out to the one that hates us.

In our Old Testament reading, the prophet Amos has an equally unpopular message to convey to the northern kingdom of Israel. A harsh word for them was given to him, and he is reprimanded and asked to go back home!

People tend to liken prophets to preachers, but I don't think that is so. We tend to expect it, but Pastors are not always prophets. Pastors, with all their training in law, are scribes. Researchers. At their best moments they are Illuminators. The congregation is called to be the prophet. The voice of the believer, the baptized, the elder, the deacon, the servant... These are the prophets. Amos gives a wonderful description in verses 14 and 15. "I'm no career preacher! I don't have a degree – I have no training! I'm a shepherd, a working man. I'm no trained scholar!" I am holding down two jobs back home – he says. Yet Amos is the one to whom this powerful word is given.

Amos is charged by God to bring something unique to the people of a place that was not his home; that was not his community.

The role of prophet isn't always a full time position. In the midst of living our lives, as Christians there will come times when we are blessed and called by God to do a special thing, to have a special word, when we are convicted to perform a special action.

The student in my youth group, those years ago, was a prophet. He answered a call that was laid on him to put forth the question to the leader, to act like Amos and make the call and say the word that was, "You know the law, but are you practicing it?" Are you doing the hard work that the law, the love of God, is requiring you to do?

Because of that young prophet, I was moved right then and there to reach out to my one time friend and make the first motions toward real reconciliation. In reality, the group wouldn't let me talk my way out of it in any way, shape, or form and weren't appeased until they watched on the big screen as I commandeered the projector's computer and wrote him the first e-mail in over six years. Those students held me accountable and checked in periodically asking for updates. The end result was full healing for my friend and me. I visited his home. I sat with his family. We talked more and overcame our enmity towards each other. We shared many meals. When the visit was over we left each other with care and friendship. We surely lost a lot that could never be recovered, but there was peace, and healing after a fashion, and the beginnings of reconciliation.

I thought I knew the law.

We must answer that call. We must be to one another and to the world – even if that world is outside our normal community – we must be the prophets. We have to make the hard line of creating a story that says, you think you know how to love, but do you really? And in the asking we may find ourselves convicted by questions that raise up from the crowd.

We may be tested like the parable of the Good Samaritan and given the opportunity to reach out to the one who we think despises us. To make that incredibly frightening move to put ourselves in front of our enemy in weakness, and depend on their love.

When we do this, when we act in this way, we are depending not on the kindness of the world, but we are trusting in the care that God is taking in our lives. We place ourselves fully outside of our own power and only in the Lord's power. And those actions, when witnessed by the world, have great strength, they become the prophet's message all on their own, and echo God's power and love for this world.

Loving the enemy and forging ahead with peace isn't about our coming from a place of power and security – because that doesn't work and requires very little faith in God on our part. Instead, the calling and the conviction of the prophet in each one of us is to accept our total *vulnerability* at the hands of our enemies, and to go out of our way to care for and honor the people who, we are sure, despise us.

This action requires our faith. This kind of action cannot be achieved apart from our total trust and reliance on God, and it is to *that* end that the church is created. The church helps the believers to trust that God is mighty, and to follow this difficult way that has been created by our Savior, our shepherd.

18
Anti-Prosperity

Written after Steven Furtick said that he deserved to live in a $1.7 million dollar mansion

HABAKKUK 1:1 - 2:4
2 THESSALONIANS 1:1-12

There is something like a dirty word that is circulating in the circles of pastors.

The phrase is "prosperity theology."

Though most often it gets shortened to a more familiar, "prosperity gospel," and when it's talked about, it is met with shaking heads and upturned mouths. It doesn't sound like something that is so bad, but, even though you are putting two great words together, the meaning behind it can be destructive.

"Prosperity Gospel" teaches that Christians are entitled to well-being and, because physical and spiritual realities are seen as one inseparable reality, this is interpreted as physical health and economic prosperity. This is incredibly dangerous territory. When we preach or witness about the Good News as if it is there for our benefit in these ways, it caters to our human desires and does not challenge us to actual discipleship and spiritual witness. It is the kind of Gospel that says, "you are going to get a big car, and a fine house, and a huge income because you are a Christian, and further, your prosperity is a marker of how great the gospel is alive in your life."

A semi-famous pastor serving in Charlotte NC has recently been in the limelight for his multi-million dollar house. Stephen Furtick, has made "prosperity theology" more well known by his obscene wealth, that he has made the gospel known by his testimony. His multi million dollar house is an 8,500 square footer set up in the woods at the end of a very long private drive. He explains that this house is a "gift" from God, and he doesn't understand what all the fuss is about. According to him it's not really "that great of a house."

Prosperity theology states that God is obviously on your side if you are successful and wealthy, which means "successful and wealthy" as measured by the standard of the world. A measurement which we need to understand is a fundamentally anti-Biblical and diseased concept of success. It always has been.

The Annual report from the church of which Furtick is a pastor has arrows and numbers decrying income, money spent on outreach, new members, new kids, even numbers on how many people they are bringing through the door, and they all have arrows - arrows going up! Up is good! God must be on our side!

Can you see the disastrous effects this line of thinking can have on us?

This sets us up in this world to expect all the good things as a direct result of our action, or rather, of our faith and God's favor toward us. God is the ultimate "vending machine" and prayer becomes nothing more than a means to choose what we want from the case at our disposal. "Prosperity Gospel" encourages people more towards selfishness and less towards a personal life with the Spirit. It brings us further from God's desire to be a people set apart as a witness to all the world by telling us that success is measured only by how the world sees it. In numbers, in cars, in houses, in clothes. It runs the dangerous risk of allowing us to lose our focus on things that are outside of our own desires because we are constantly checking to see if our desires are being met as the measuring rod of our apostolic worth.

Perhaps Habakkuk is asking a question after witnessing something similar. He knows there is something off about the way in which he has to live through injustice. He wants a certain amount of worldly success.

How do we reconcile the fact that God promises action, and what could very well be favor to the faithful, without edging toward that understanding that God really is moving in the world to get us that new car, or that really good parking spot? How do we further allow ourselves to cry out in complaint against God without being completely selfish?

Habakkuk does one thing immediately right. He is asking the Lord for help, or rather is asking how long the wait must be. In this simple beginning, Habakkuk is acknowledging the power and sovereignty that God has over his world and over his life. He knows that help comes from God, and that God is the master of the timing in which that will take place.

That back and forth, that tension between honesty and selfishness takes place.

The prophet asks in the last part of the first chapter how God tolerates people who "deal treacherously," and those who keep silent as real evil and harm swallow up righteous people. Where is a little of the good life for the faithful?! In the next chapter he waits for God to respond to this challenge, and God says that in God's own time evil people will be judged and infinitely more harshly. "Woe to those," says the Creator of the Universe and all things, "Woe to people who get an evil gain for their house."

I wonder how Furtick would place Habakkuk and God's reply.

God is saying that the bad times, these times of devastation and exile in Habakkuk's life, are being used for God's purpose. That success is not at all a measure of God's presence with his people, or of the finality that they will be met with. In fact, those who are wealthy and in power and placed over many servants are going to be the first to feel God's wrath through the destruction brought by the invading Babylonian Empire. A reckoning is coming.

Habakkuk's reply later in chapter 3 is to express his ultimate faith in God, even if he doesn't fully understand. In 3:17 he says, "For though the fig tree doesn't flourish, nor fruit be in the vines; the labor of the olive fails, the fields yield no food; the flocks are cut off from the fold, and there is no herd in the stalls." In the very next verse however he says, "yet I will rejoice in Yahweh. I will be joyful in the God of my salvation!" Joy in God's will in our lives, God's presence in our lives and God's hand in our lives *does not hinge* on our public favor and success. Lives led in excess, exploiting and showing off the riches of comfort in this world, doing nothing to progress our discipleship or witness to the world, and in fact work to erode it.

Paul describes the currency that is paid out for righteousness: faith and love for one another. Not riches to make life easier, or to hire troops to protect them. Not plentiful food, or chariots so that they can overcome their enemies and establish themselves in places of power. None of that. Simply more faith and love for one another. *That* is the way in which the people of God can boast and know that God is a right and good Judge of the world. Not any other way. Not arrows going up in numerical gain, but arrows going out reaching in love to one another.

So what about our cars? Our houses, our savings? What part is human hubris and what part is Godly gift? When things go wrong, is God punishing our idolatry? When things are blessed, are we pleasing to God?

There are two things at work.

One is the fact that real evil exists in the world. We can act in righteousness and still suffer under the actions of evil people. In Habakkuk, God outlines the woes of Israel as they are profiting from the poor, creating poverty and wasting their own wealth for personal pleasure. Even if we are faithful, there is no guarantee that we will escape all worldly corruption.

The second is that sometimes Christians prosper, but can we say that it is God's doing? Is it possible that this is why we become so disenchanted with God, so angry as Habakkuk was, when things don't go the way we expected. I have lived a good life God! Why do this to me? We had a thriving ministry! Why take it away from us?

God is not powerless, but works in a way that runs counter to our human expectations. Which is why it requires so much from us to have trust and faith in God. Daily bread in the early church was dependent on the sharing that took place between believers. And that's all we pray for. Proverbs 30:9 is a prayer that asks for not poverty or wealth. In poverty we die and curse God, and in riches we forget who God is.

We expect things, stuff, to fill our lives and to make our day more pleasant. God responds with Faith and Love for one another. Those are the things that are the most valuable, and though God answers Habakkuk, the response is, just wait. Trust me. I will take care of the very important things.

Sometimes it's so hard, because we want success for Jesus! We want to show the world that being a Christian is rewarding, and so does God. It's just the difference between the human and the divine reward.

If you sing the hymn "Come thou Font" you can see what blessings are mentioned there. It isn't one that includes cars, and success, and fame, and people chanting your name in a crowd. It asks for Faith, and love for each other and our God. That is the reward that "tunes our hearts," and "fixes us on the mount of Heaven." This song encourages us against the kind of church that is obsessed with numbers and arrows and thinks that their pastor deserves a multi-million dollar home. The only reward they see is in the physicality of this place. The money, the house, the fame. The true font of blessing is working to make an interwoven and re-enforced web of love and faith between the people of God, so that when those inevitable evils of the universe fall on us, we know there is a family we can depend on. We know that there is a God who is caring for us better than the best investments we could ever make. That is what makes up the "melodious sonnet" from the hymn.

We sometimes find it so hard to get over our disappointment, our places of injury in this world, and we think that the only way to get over these things is to get them later. If we get passed over for a job, well, another even *better* job is waiting for us. We missed out on a money making opportunity? Well, even *more* money stands to be made. Hurt by friends? Well, we will have *better* friends at other places.

The truth is that God's way of healing these slights and injuries free us from human desire and shackle us to God instead. We don't have to wait for a better job, or more money, or the extra special friends. We are supplied by God in the here and now, and if that doesn't seem like enough it is only our human hearts wanting more.

But it is enough.

Trust God.

Learn the "melodious sonnet" like a mantra and repeat it.

19
Perceivable Newness

Written after the death of actress Carrie Fisher and astronomer Vera Rubin

ROMANS 8:22-30
JERIMIAH 1:4-10

If you are part of the space loving community, then this past week was hard for you. Not only did the actress who played Leia Organa Solo (Carrie Fisher) finally succumb to complications from her heart attack, but we also lost one of my favorite astrophysicists who passed as well; Vera Rubin. Hopefully you are at least familiar with the role of Princess Leia (who later became a general) from the Star Wars movie universe, but it's possible you are less familiar with Dr. Rubin, who was an amazing mind in our own universe.

Dr. Rubin is responsible for our understanding of an enormous problem in the universe: the fact that galaxies don't move right.

In essence, she discovered that if a galaxy only relied on the gravity of the stars contained within them, that they should instead be flinging solar systems into the starry heavens like nuts and bolts from a cheap carnival ride. She knew there had to be some other, yet unobservable mass, holding things together. This discovery was, and still is today, the greatest mathematically provable argument for the existence of dark matter in the universe, which is calculated to comprise almost a third of the universal mass.

It's strange and somehow poetic that both these women should pass within a week of each other. In the fictional Star Wars universe, Leia fought against an evil empire with courage and care using her status as a leader to free the galaxy from oppression. She was no ordinary princess. She wielded a blaster pistol, and though she was rescued - technically - at one point by Luke and Han, she didn't melt into a doe-eyed gooey pile of a distressed damsel. She grabbed a weapon and led the charge. Throughout her story, she is incredibly strong and later became a general in what was the new government of the galaxy. Not a diplomat. Not a senator. A general.

Within a year of Star Wars coming out in 1977, Vera Rubin was publishing her findings on the galactic rotation problem. She had long fought against the oppression of another male dominated system. For instance, she earned entry to Princeton for graduate work, but was shut out of the astronomy program because of her gender. She never stopped though, and worked bravely and truly against their misogyny and published a groundbreaking document that forever changed how we see Newtonian physics playing out in the universe.

Space has always been a place of inspiration for me, partially because of the astronomy lessons my dad gave me and my brother growing up; teaching us the names of the Galilean moons circling Jupiter, following the status of Voyager and the shuttle launches. When the Hubble telescope went up in 1990, that was a big day for the Tweel kids. So, for anyone who finds space inspiring and incredible, these deaths have, as a friend of mine put it, "Left some big shoes and blaster holsters to fill in the world."

In contemplating the lives of these women together, I see something interesting rise to the surface. Something that is perhaps the reason why we find their lives so captivating, and their story so hopeful. They led lives of struggle. True, one was fictional, but both of these lives were tales of stout bravery, and of commitment, and tenacity.

As humans we usually balk, or turn from times of struggle and, well, speaking for myself, tend to complain a lot when stuff isn't going our own way. It's part of our condition and how our brains are wired. We desire ease and comfort, even though it's not really what's best for us. There was an old Garfiled comic that said, in truth, "sloth was the mother of invention." Which might be closer to the point. We invent things to make life easier. In reality our bodies were made to live in the roughness of the world, even though our brains were built to drive us into creating a more comfortable system.

For instance; a New Year tradition the world over is to take some kind of plunge into icy water. It has different names depending on where you are, but all the northern climates of the world do the same thing. They find a frozen lake, and they jump in.

Now our brains are going to tell us that is crazy! But our bodies actually respond in a really healthy way to this. The cold shock to the system jump-starts the lymphatic system which is responsible for (among other things) clearing out the junk that lodges in our systems. It works with the blood and kidneys and liver, to remove toxins. And after a winter season of doing minimal physical labor, and perhaps eating richer foods, these shock treatment traditions, in the middle of winter have real health benefits. We can mimic the same thing by taking a cold shower after a steam bath, or just splashing cold water on our faces in the morning.

But the thing is - we don't want to take a cold shower. We want to lie in a warm bed. Crank that electric blanket up to 100, drink some tea, watch a movie, and slowly sink down into a twilight consciousness of warm happiness.

Yet, we are healthier jumping into the cold and daunting waters for a few seconds.

In that light, I was looking at this reading from Romans. Paul says that the Spirit helps us in our weakness. It's interesting that I don't think Paul actually says something that we all might assume; that this 'support in weakness' purpose is to make us strong. That it is to somehow alter us to a new form that no longer requires the Spirit's intercession.

Isn't that how we think? That we are weak, made stronger by God and then go on to face the world of sin somehow stronger? Different? So that in the next challenge we will not be cowed or, it follows, be as reliant on God? In some kind of strange habit, it feels as if we think that God's intent is to strengthen us until we simply don't need God's intercession any longer. That we can stand on our own two feet for the purposes of Christ and move mountains.

That isn't what Paul is saying.

There is something inherently wrong with that view of how God acts and expects us to act. There is something missing. I think we are forgetting our own dark matter.

Note that what Paul is saying is different from saying that we struggle, or have tragedy in life *in order to* make us stronger. As if a loving God would purposefully inflict trauma or harm on us in order to teach us a lesson. That's human thinking, and not the way a God that sacrifices a child for salvation would behave.

Instead, Paul is stating a fact, a condition of what it is to be human. Not a lacking piece of *some* Christians, but a perfunctory measure of what it is to *be* human. We are weak. We will always be weak. We will never be any other way. Period.

We contain dark matter.

It's how our galaxy functions.

It's the only way it works.

Previous to this Paul is saying that creation has groaned for what has come, and that we wait for adoption and the redemption of our bodies. This is interesting because it hints at a very complicated understanding that Paul has when it comes to our salvation. Paul first says that creation exists in a new way right now. Then he says that we still wait and groan for the redemption of our bodies. He then follows that with verse 24, "Because in, or by, Hope we are saved."

If we read too quickly we miss it. Creation has changed. The universe is fundamentally different in the now. But we are still waiting for adoption. Our likeness to the universe is in comparing our yearning. However unlike the universe, our salvation comes through hope, which, as it turns out is a tricky thing.

It's possible that we have read that before and thought that, yes, I had a hope in being saved and then I was saved, and now I am saved, and so - I don't need that hope any longer. I am done with that kind of hope, that groaning, birth-pang, waiting for blessed adoption hope. That has passed.

I don't think that's true.

Paul goes on to explain, hope that is seen is not hope. If we feel like we have been saved and have no need for that kind of hope, then we have *seen*, we have *felt*, we have *experienced*. Paul says that *isn't* hope. Paul says we hope for what we *do not* see.

Now this is present tense grammar structure, a perfect time for the rigidity of Greek to take a hold of us. This isn't a metaphoric time structure; it's a rigid continuing present. This is Paul's current reality and the reality he expects for all other Christians until the end of time. A state of constant Hope for the unseen, unknown, unknowable true heart of God.

A hope that is eternally unresolved and tied to our salvation.

To us, here in our 21st century world of finite concepts and T.V. shows that publish entire seasons at once, this probably seems like the worst thing ever.

We want to say, "That's not the way hope works Paul, you hope something happens, then it happens, then you get rewarded with happiness and dopamine." That isn't what Paul is saying.

It sounds crazy, but Paul hinges his whole understanding of who Christians are on it. We are the people of the "yet to come." The children of the "Soon to be Returning King." We aren't people of victory in that way, we're people of hope. We are a people of waiting.

It feels better to be people who win though. It feels better to have our little pleasure centers in our brain to be able to tell the world that we've won, and that the bad people of the world are our enemies, and they have lost. Which isn't any kind of real Christianity.

Maybe it seems hard to be people locked into a perpetual state of hope. A people whose salvation depends on our patient waiting; which is why I added this verse from Jeremiah.

A lot of times this verse gets read to young students as a way of saying, "Hey, look here, God picked a young prophet, you can be a prophet too, God doesn't discount the young people." While that is technically true, in reality, God pretty much always called young people. If anything we should be going to the older folks and showing them examples of prophets who were called while they were older, of whom there are fewer.

I picked this passage for the very important things God has to say to Jeremiah in verse 5. God knew who Jeremiah was. That's the reason Jeremiah is called to do the work that he has to do. Because God knows Jeremiah so intimately, and so profoundly, that God is absolutely sure that this is the right person for the job. Of course Jeremiah's immediate response is to tell God the error of such a notion. So the issue is this; when we think that the life that God has outlined for us, or the calling we have, is too much, or too crazy, or too hard, we don't have to imagine that our choices are either to one, buck up and gain power and strength or to just grit our teeth through it until it's over.

The truth, and the blessed alternative, is that the strength we need will be there, *is* there in fact, and always *was* because God knew it was there from the very beginning. That's how well God knows us.

Being people of Hope is a difficult task. It means that we don't get to win. It means that there are no triumphal marches or parades and medals pinned to our human chests in this life. It means knowing that there is no exit from our weakness, except that we are constantly buoyed up by the function of the Spirit to intercede on our behalf.

When we stay in bed under the covers, we think we are made to be perpetually warm, when really, the shock of the frozen river and harshness of the world gets our blood pumping.

So here's a radical idea.

We're better Christians when we don't get what we want. If we consider our endless state of weakness as Paul says, what we *want* should never come to pass.

Would Princess Leia have been the driving inspirational leader that she becomes if she lived in one of the rich neighborhoods of Alderan that was catered to her whole life? Would Rubin have been so driven by her own ideas if she had simply been accepted into the "Good Old Boy" system of the late 70's?

We are better Christians, we are truer Christians, when we exist and accept our existence in a perpetual state of Hope. That's hard for us because we live in a universe which caters to our desire for resolution and gratification. It's a system we have to see as unhealthy.

We tend to cry out to God when we don't get our way. We have this systematic and sick ideology that teaches us, *against* what Paul is saying here, that we earn our blessings by being good people, or being polite, or being part of the status quo and not making "trouble."

Yet these are the things that Paul is considering as our inherent weakness.

The things that come easy to us are the things that we are already programmed to do. We want to sit in bed and be warm. Yet the Spirit intercedes, and refuses to allow us to sit and stagnate. We commit our lives to Christ, and our time as purely weak Christians is over -- in so much as we allow the Spirit of God to cast us out into the frozen water. We are not supposed to have our hope achieved and wrapped up in a nice little bow. We are supposed to live in a world of wonder. A system of unresolved hope in a God we do not understand, but yet have met with faith in our hearts.

The most wonderful thing about dark matter is how little we know about it. We aren't even sure if we *can* know anything about it as our human perception is confined to a system based on the electromagnetic structure of the other two thirds of the universe. The electromagnetic spectrum is a system of energy in our universe that does everything from making our power, examining our bones, giving us a tan and relaying our communication across the globe. Everything we see with our eyes is only a narrow band of that electromagnetic field.

Dark matter *isn't* a part of that structure.

It doesn't respond at all to any portion of the electromagnetic field, but it has mass. It's a quandary. An enigma that uses up one third of the universe[25] and is responsible (most likely) for keeping our galaxies from flying apart into the void of space. We might never know anything more about it. And that makes us better astrophysicists.

Our place as hopeful people makes us better Christians. We are at our worst as Christians when we get what we want, because, as Paul knows, we are best when we know that we are weak, supported constantly in every way by the Spirit of the Lord and perpetually hopeful about a God we know little about.

So I pray that we will meet our lives with no sense of misplaced victory, but instead with a sense of Hope. I pray that we will not be met with the things we want. Instead, I pray that we will better become those people of that Hope. The Hope through which Paul says we are saved.

Only something as unknowable as dark matter can keep the universe together.

Only people of Hope can truly affect this world for God's real and powerful Kingdom.

---

[25] Rubin, Vera C. *Bright Galaxies, Dark Matters*. Masters of Modern Physics. Woodbury, N.Y.: American Institute of Physics, 1997

20
Surrounded by Death

Written after serving as a chaplain at a local hospital

JOHN 11:1-44

Dr. Ken Kalmer is an orthopedic microsurgeon who was a witness to death on the slopes of Mount Everest in 1996. This particular climb goes down in history as one of the deadliest moments ever in Everest's history and carries with it a harrowing tale.

We can listen in on this story through his book "Doctor on Everest[26]" where he talks about their expedition looking at winds that were so high that the temperature on the summit was colder than it would have been on a summer's day on the planet Mars. This team was full of seismic researchers and IMAX photographers. Seasoned hikers all, they were even hosted by the Explorer's Club. Ken's book makes a great narrative as he describes the team in 1996 moving over a series of days from the base camp, which is at 17,000 feet, to the summit which is almost more than twice that height at 29,000 feet. If you have done any hiking and climbed even 1,000 feet in elevation, you know that it is a daunting walk.

To move from base camp to camp one, the team had to climb over an ice flow; which is an enormous frozen waterfall which changes its configuration *every day* due to it melting and refreezing. They climb this at night, when the ice is more solidly frozen and has less chance of breaking loose. From there, it is on to camp two, three, four and finally the summit. It is a journey battling ten-story crevasses, exhaustion, altitude sickness, and dehydration, not to mention the hourly battle with the frigid temperature and monitoring oxygen levels. Even the Summit of Everest is in a jet stream, and to reach it, you climb through the cloud layer. With all of these factors, the ascent of Everest is actually the easier part of the trip.

The last long climb to the summit, however, is a solo climb -- which is to say that none of the climbers are roped to each other. The reason for this is that the drop offs to either side are so sheer that falling and being tied to someone else would simply drag them off with you.

If you fall off to your right, on the last few miles of hiking, you go 8000 feet to Nepal, if you fell to your left, it was 12000 feet to Tibet. Which as Ken

---

[26] Doctor on Everest by Kenneth Kamler, Lyons Press, 2000

says in the book, "is the better option because you will live longer - but either way you fall for the rest of your life."

On this climb that took place in 1996, and while the summit team were still on the ridge, the worst storm Ken had ever seen, whipped up around the mountain. The winds were so fierce that they were piling all their gear in the center of the tent and lying on top of it to keep the tents from being blown away.

While they were hunkered down during the storm, a torrent of confused radio reports came in from the climbers who were still on the ridge. They were lost, confused and unable to find shelter. There were eighteen climbers in that mess of snow and ice.

After the worst of it had passed, two of the strongest climbers in Camp Three left to try and help the lost in any way they could. Ken overheard a radio transmission between these rescue climbers and another climber, Rob Paul, who weathered the storm and had a radio on him. They said that he would need to "leave Doug [his climbing partner, who was a weaker and less experienced climber] and come down, there's no chance to save him, so save yourself." As Ken says; "Rob received that message over the radio, but his reply was, 'we're both listening.'"

Doug ended up dying on the mountain, even though the other hikers got to him before he passed.

Doug could not be moved. His frostbite had gotten to the point where he couldn't make it down and being carried across the narrow treacherous terrain was physically impossible. He asked for his radio transmission to be patched back to his wife, however, so he could say his farewells. His wife was still in New Zealand and pregnant, yet this allowed them to speak with each other for the last time and name their unborn daughter together.

The next piece of news they heard was that the rescue climbers had come upon Beck Weathers, a seasoned climber, who had collapsed in the snow and was dead. At Camp Three, Ken and the others on the support team for this climb, were busy preparing as best they could to receive anyone who made it with the meager medical supplies they had with them at that high altitude.

"Oh Lord, if you had *been* here..."

Martha's initial word to Jesus sounds an awful lot like accusation.

Mary, after she has come out of the house, repeats the same thing, "If you had been here Lord..."

I think these phrases sound like accusations because we readily identify with these sisters in their moment of grief. We know the story that their grief tells, we have felt it and we have perhaps called out that same phrase. "If you had been here Lord..."

When I was serving as one of the chaplains at Memorial Regional over in Mechanicsville, Virginia, I said that phrase. I accused God, I shook my head, I gritted my teeth.

One night on-call, I was paged and I made my way down to the emergency room. One of the attending nurses filled me in: a pregnant woman had just come in, she was so far non-responsive and had passed out while riding in her van after having dinner out with her family. Her father, mother and three-year-old daughter were in the consult room; they were trying to get a hold of her husband who was out of town on business.

I went into the consult room and sat with them. In verse 20 of John, it says that Mary stayed at home, but this is really a "sitting" at home, a reference to the Jewish understanding of being "in place" with one's grief. Dying is outside of the normal motions of life, and the Jewish response to this is to be "sat with" by members of the community. In the Hospital consult room, the adults were in a frantic questioning buzz, a pre-grief mood, it was an electrically charged and worried place. I talked with them briefly and asked if any of them wanted to walk with me in the garden while we waited for the emergency room team to get back to us.

The grandmother, the little three-year-old and I went out. The grandfather, the injured woman's father, stayed to try and raise the husband on the phone. We walked in the garden, and I found herbs planted there for the daughter to smell, trying to distract her a little. The grandmother was also on the phone, when the little girl told me, with a heart full of trust and belief, "My momma is here with the doctors who are going to make her feel better."

It breaks your heart.

I couldn't give her an affirmative agreement because I had seen the nurses' faces only minutes before. So, instead, I told her that she didn't have to worry because her grandparents and her Dad had such a big love for her. I couldn't tell her that the last thing I had heard from the emergency team was that they were trying to save the baby. So I told her that I knew, without a doubt, that her momma loved her so very much. I couldn't tell her that they were adamant in getting a hold of the father... just in case the worst happened. So I asked her to tell me how she felt about all this.

After a while of talking and playing in the fountain I led them back inside, and we waited a bit longer, we prayed, and talked a little more before I had to go on to another patient. When I had a minute to circle back around to them, their home pastor was with them. Both the mother and the baby had died. I didn't go in to see them again. I couldn't face that little girl, and I knew I didn't have to with their family pastor there now, so I slipped away.

I went back out into the garden, and wept.

Jesus weeps in this passage.

It's not the same weeping that he has over the city. This word in Greek means a *silent weeping*. A deep emotion that falls in quiet tears. This might seem odd, because we imagine that Jesus knows Lazarus is going to be raised. Why is he sad? I read all kinds of complicated theories about why this is. Some question the extent of Jesus's power, or his connection to God weakening while still experiencing human pain, or the faith of others affecting the power of miracles. I have come to this conclusion: Jesus weeps because Jesus has emotional empathy. Even as incarnate God in the Old Testament we are told that God has emotions. In Jeremiah 48, God "wails for Moab." In Genesis 6, "the heart of God grieves." In Psalm 103, "God has a parental compassion for us," and the list could go on. God is jealous, joyful, angry - is it so incredible that the reason Jesus cries here is because it is sad to lose someone? Because others are weeping? Because Jesus is sharing in that moment of pain with them? Isn't that what we do for one another?

As Mary, whom Jesus loves, and all the others are weeping, so too does Jesus weep. Because God knows our emotions. Because God cares for his people.

In the garden at the hospital, I wept and I was also accusing. "If you had only been here, Lord." If you had only heard my prayer, or the prayer of that little girl.

If you had only been here, Lord.

That storm wouldn't have come so quickly, those men would not have frozen to death.

That baby and her mother would still be alive.

We would have a place to live.

The church in America wouldn't be in this mess.

My spouse would not have left.

My job would not have been lost.

That accident wouldn't have been so bad.

My children wouldn't have been killed in their school.

I would have gotten into the right college, gotten the right job, experienced success, felt needed and loved...

If you had only been here Lord.

We do this. Perhaps that makes it seem easy for us to read Martha's statement as the same kind of thing.

But, it isn't the same thing.

Mary and Martha are accepting what is. Martha, yet, has faith beyond that of her sister. She is stating what exists in the present time, but this phrase is inexorably tied to the second part of the phrase. It is in effect a factual expression of her future faith. The sentence "If you had been here," is only possible because of the stalid faith that is present in the second half of that phrase, "...even now I know God will give you, will do for you, will be done, as you say it will be." The grammar of the Greek ties these two phrases. The word, *kai*, is one of the first words we ever learned in Greek. It's an article that is used all over the place and is used to mean *and, also, even, indeed, but* - it can be used interchangeably to some degree based on the surrounding grammar. So read those verses again. "He wouldn't have died had you been here Lord, and I know that God will grant to you whatever you ask."

It's not a statement of accusal but of belief. It's not even something that is conditional, "Raise him and I will believe." It's one total statement of fact and faith. Everything else that follows in the conversation with Jesus isn't a test of the faith of Martha because she accused Jesus of tardiness, but a conversation of affirmation.

"Do you believe this?"

"Of course I believe it! You are the Christ! The eternal life giver! It would have been impossible for our brother to die if you had been here because you are life. You are here now, and I know that whatever you desire will happen."

She doesn't demand Jesus raise him. This is a statement of trust and faith that lays the action of what comes next wholly in her Lord's hands.

Mary isn't there yet. She's not as firm in her faith at this moment. She knows that had Jesus been there he wouldn't have died, but she doesn't attach the same second phrase that Martha does. But Jesus doesn't get frustrated with her lack of faith. He weeps with her. He doesn't condemn her. He is moved by her.

We can be in one of three places when surrounded by death, by loss, by even just the pain of our own lives gone wrong. The place of Martha, secure in knowing who God is and "all in" by way of placing the action in God's hand. The place of Mary, faithful in whom the sovereign of life is but still caught in her emotion, supported by Jesus Christ. Or the third place. The most human place. The place of accusal, lashing out to blame God for every wrong in our world.

On the slopes of Everest, still high in the clouds, Dr Ken was treating people in a small tent for severe frostbite and hypothermic dementia[27] for several days. After this period, still at Camp Three, Beck Weathers, who had been pronounced dead by two other climbers, walked into the tent, alive, and having walked there on his own to open the tent and ask, "Where should I sit Ken? I hope you take my insurance."

Beck had gotten lost, and collapsed in the snow during the storm. He had heard the other climbers say "he's dead" and unable to move, unable to even blink, laid there for a day, a night, and another whole day. After that, he says, thinking about his family and the people he loved, against all reason and medical understanding, he got up and walked miles through the night and through the snow, and found Camp Three where Dr. Ken and his medical rescue team were waiting.

---

[27] Hypothermia can cause confused thinking and prevents self-awareness. The confused thinking can also lead to risk-taking behavior.

They rescued fourteen of those eighteen hikers and for those who couldn't hike back down from Camp Three, they carried them out to meet the highest altitude helicopter rescue in history.

Not everyone survived that trip. Not every woman and unborn baby survives the night. Not every division is healed by our prayer. Our lives often do not take the easy path. Mary and Martha's brother died.

When this is the case, we must know that God cares, and in Jesus Christ, weeps. Our pain is not callously cast into the void, unlooked upon by an unconcerned Creator. When this painful life is the case, we have a choice to make. We can, as we have in the past, accuse God of uncaring. Of simply witnessing our death and struggle, of being aloof to our lives. But this does nothing for us.

Or, we can like Mary, admit that when God -- when Christ -- comes near, that life is undeniable. Life is inescapable. Because Jesus Christ is the Lord of resurrection and life, and can still weep. Knowing that there is no rebuke from Christ in this action.

Or, we can, like Martha, know deeply in us that Jesus Christ is the only Messiah, the one who brings life out of death, and that even in our sadness, even as we rail at the rank injustice of this world, we can be assured that the Son of God has come into this place to save us.

None of these choices alter our experience with death. What it does do is alter our continued experience with life. That's who we are. People of life. People who, though surrounded by death and tears, are not defined by that pain even as we sit with it. We are not called to ignore it or to stuff it away, but we are also not called to allow it to become who we are.

Dr. Ken Kalmer, Mary, Martha and all of us - we have been witness to death, witness to pain. Yet we are called to become witnesses of life and resurrection because we believe in the Messiah, the Son of God, the one who has come into the world as the bringer of Life.

21
Hospitable Ears

Written as I was seeking a new call into ministry

GENESIS 3:1-9
MARK 15:33-41

The death of Jesus isn't something we often connect with.

The real death, not the concept.

The real, gritty, last words of Christ shouted into the sky kind of death.

It has its usual place in the yearly schedule. Around Easter or sometimes even Christmas, we dust off the passages about the end of Jesus' earthly life and read them with somber quietness. It seems like the right thing to do. In this passage from Mark, we are with Jesus at the cross. There is death and darkness. Tearing and pain. There is tragedy. There is a *mighty* shout. There are women who love Jesus standing apart. It's pretty depressing. Every movie, every passion play, or musical portrays the scene in the same way. A tangible sense of hurt and weeping and pain. It's no wonder that we do not often meditate on this verse. It's no wonder that it gets relegated to the theatrics of our High Holy celebrations. It's gruesome.

So let's do something else.

Let's start out with a story instead. How about I tell you a little bit about one of my favorite people in the world? My grandmother.

We called her Sittie, which is just the Arabic slang term for grandma. She was from Damascus and even though she grew up in Brooklyn, New York, she held all of those awesome traits of Middle Eastern hospitality. She smoked, but only outside, and cursed in Arabic thinking that the grandkids didn't know what she was saying. She served her church faithfully for decades, and I always loved going to worship with her Episcopal congregation when we were in town. She played pranks on her friends and had an amazing laugh. And, she was best known for her cooking. Her hands, I loved her hands, they always smelled like onions and garlic. People would tell her all the time that she could open her own restaurant. I would follow her into the kitchen, starting when I was young. We listened to old jazz standards on the radio as we ground meat and added spices to various dishes. She would show me technique and a love for making food that lasts to this day. It was how she shared a deep love with the world. Every dish told a story. She could smell something and know if it needed more salt. She would crack jokes, and we would laugh as she ate bits of raw meat, to make sure it was fresh. I would watch and obey her intently, and eventually as I learned, I would help her prepare. Endless dishes for a banquet of royalty came out of her kitchen each with its own crafted smell and taste and would be placed on her enormous wooden table. Her house was my favorite place.

To come into my grandmother's house was to be, in a way, accosted by hospitality. You literally could not escape without having at least a cup of coffee, and everything was offered three times.

"Have a cup of coffee. Just, one cup! Come on, I just brewed it fresh. Well, now that you have coffee, you can't have just coffee. You want something to go with it, right?" It was like a vaudevillian bit she did with everyone who came over. And people came over all the time. You were lavished with attention and treats and anything else you wanted. We were all used to it of course. It felt warm and cozy. As my cousins and I dated and married outside the Arab culture however, we began to see how people were really put off by it. It became a misinterpretation of kindness and great love to be anxious when our Sittie came at you with coffee service and boston cream pie.

My daughter notices it with my dad now.

Our house tends to be quieter. I'm a pretty gregarious guy, but our hospitality is more subtle and genial. Dad's is still very ethnically loud a lot of the time, which I love and expect. That loudness feels like home to me. My daughter asked me at one point why Grandpop was yelling at her all the time to eat. I had to laugh and tell her, when you hear Grandpop say those things, just imagine he is saying "I love you so much!" because really that is what he means. That reframing for her seemed to do the trick. So, now, after the second or third time he offers her a snack that she doesn't really want and has already said no to, she just says, "I love you, too."

When the love is greater than we expect, we often have to retune our ears to hear the real story, so that something that was once abrasive sounds deeply loving. Something that was once an affront, feels like home. Something that was once tragic is instead a moment of powerful joy.

We read this verse from Mark all wrong. This verse should be read with joy. With praise and with gladness -- and we get that, right? On some level, we always hear the triumph of Easter brass playing behind the tympanic thunder of Good Friday. We know that our *real* identity is one of "Easter People," and yet we still miss the larger message of this passage. The joyful message. It's not hidden. Jesus himself tells us exactly where to look - in a place we usually see only pain and defeat.

"Eloi, eloi, lama sabachthani"
"My God, my god. Why have you forsaken me?"

These are the words of victory.

These last words of Christ? They are not a lament. They are a quote.

We only have to look to Psalm 22 to see the story.

This psalm starts out with this *same* line. In fact, the Greek words used in Mark are the exact same words ascribed to the psalm in the Septuagint: the Greek translation of the Hebrew scriptures. If we put ourselves in the place of the author, this psalm begins asking "why have you forsaken me?" but it doesn't *only* say that. It is not *only* a lament.

It is not *only* a questioning of why God has pulled far away from the author.

It is not *only* crying out into the darkness: it is a pledge of hope and trust.

Halfway through this psalm, it talks about the way in which God has brought us safely through our own birth, and how we have been cared for since the day we were born, and it talks of *rescue*. Rescue from enemies who encircle us and seek to consume us utterly. Enemies who sneer and gamble for our possessions as they are auctioned off. This should sound familiar to the story of the Cross of Christ.

Still, these greedy dogs who were going to kill us are *defeated* in this psalm by a God who hears and listens when the cry goes out. The psalm ends with the notion that everyone on earth will remember the truth about who God is, and about how even people who are not yet born will be told that, "it was the Lord who saved us."

And it all starts with the line; "...why have you forsaken me?"

It's not a cry for help from the cross.

It is a laughing cliff note of victory to all of those who believe.

Usually, we think that this scene is either one of Jesus' humanity coming to bear, or that in the presence of Sin, God had to be distant. That's what our media tells us. Every movie. Every play. Every musical I have ever seen has gotten that truth dead wrong. Jesus isn't having a failing moment of humanity, and God has *never* drawn away from sin in the history of existence.

Why then? Why do we get this story wrong?

It is because we have a hospitality problem.

We cannot fathom that this scene of death and woe is really one of power and victory.

We, as a human people, are bad at bearing witness to God's generosity.

We have been this way since the very beginning.

Consider the serpent in the garden, this entity of enmity, who is testing humanity in its first moments. The serpent asks, "Did God tell you not to eat from *any* tree in the garden?" And the woman corrects him; "No, no, that's wrong. God told us that we could eat the fruit of any tree in the garden, *except* the one in the middle. If we do, then we will die."

The serpent tells the truth at this point. The serpent doesn't lie. Exactly what the serpent says will happen, happens: They learn the difference between Good and Evil, they know what God knows, and they are changed utterly forever. For the record, God doesn't lie either. For God, the universe is binary in our relationship with God. Either we are alive in the presence of God, or we are dead. Only God contains life.

So, what is God's reaction to this first Sin? Does God draw away? Quite the opposite:

God calls out, "Where are you?"

God never drew away from us. God never has drawn away from us. Yes, we can *feel* that separation, *we* can be distant, but this isn't God's doing. From the very beginning of creation, from our first mistake in the garden, we drew away from God. And hid. Because we were afraid. God instantly reached out to find us.

This is our hospitality problem. Misinterpreting God's goodness as God keeping something from us. God giving us everything we could want and something in us is still wanting more until we are our own gods.

There is something in us that cannot get over seeing a 'blessing' not meant for us, and not desiring to claim it. We miss the fundamental element that the good looking fruit in the middle doesn't preclude us from having every other fruit. It is repeated throughout scripture.

This is the story of Cain and Abel.

Cain hears God's favor for Abel as a threat to his own blessing in life, even though God says at that moment, "keep doing what is good and right and you will also inherit this."

This is the story of Jacob and Esau.

Jacob who could not handle his brother's elder status and so stole and tricked him and had to work endlessly to right God's will for the world.

This is the story of Joseph and his brothers, who could not see that the blessings on their brother would one day save every member of their family from death through brutal starvation.

The story of Eve and Adam who cannot see the rest of creation that is theirs to sustain them, because they cannot handle a God who knows more than they do.

The story of Jesus on the Cross, whose last words must be about God abandoning us, because we cannot easily fathom a God who will not leave us.

Over and over and over, the witness of our Biblical forbearers tell us the story of humans missing God's abundance, and instead coveting the blessing that isn't ours because we cannot trust God to be God. We are so afraid that we will miss out on the blessing, on the goodness, on the 'fact' that we have to do for ourselves, that we completely miss the deep hospitality God has for us.

It's easier to not believe that.

It's easier for us to just depend on our own strength. To store up our fortune. To protect our own communities from the unknown. To chase our own careers. To throw up borders or ordinances in order to keep what we have here. To store up mana for the next day and the next, because "what if there isn't enough? What if I can't trust God to be the only one who knows what Good and Evil are? What if God really forsakes me someday because of my sin?"

It is a sickness of inward focus that is doomed to drive us out of Eden and causes us to miss the victory of Christ.

We portray the last words of Christ with pain and torment instead of glad joy because we fail to trust in the complete holiness of Jesus Christ, Messiah of the world. Because it's impossible. It doesn't make sense.

Our God's generosity.

The real nature of God.

The reality declared to people yet unborn, the victory - it doesn't make sense.

Still, God keeps teaching us the lesson.

For every time we reach for the fruit that we covet, every time we lose sight of our beautiful image, every time we fail in the path of sin and death, what does God DO?

God seeks us out. Asks where we are. Makes clothes for us, and spends the rest of eternity saving us. That's the story of the fruit in the garden. It began there at that tree, with human mistrust and harmful desire, then spends thousands of years with a God who pursues us, chases us down relentlessly and finishes with another tree; a Son laughing and grinning and quoting well-known song lyrics of victory. The victory that is proclaimed to children yet unborn.

That's a kind of generosity and hospitality that we don't naturally have. It's a generosity that we have to relentlessly chase as well. It's a generosity that covers us when we are the ones who kill each other out of envy. When we refuse to care for people we think have led a life of overindulgence. When we won't pay our laborers in a way that is Godly. When we pursue wealth or power and make excuses. When we fail to see the truth of God's victory. The generosity of God covers us, thankfully, blessedly, when our self-righteousness steals God's image from our own faces.

When we live without trust in God and/or without understanding the depth of the abundance that God has for us, our lives feel incomplete and dark. We feel the shame of our actions, see our own nakedness, and we hide. We cry out, "My God, why have you left me?" We live *only* in the first half of Psalm 22. Instead of being left there, we are pursued by a God who says, "my child my child, why have you abandoned *me*?" We are invited to a table of trust to share a meal together. We are called to eat and be satisfied, we are asked to re-tune our ears to hear the reality of God.

When that understanding of God is ours, then in those times we are crucified. In those places, the people who hate us surround us like devouring dogs, then we will be filled with peace and powerfully recite not the first words Psalm 22, but the last: "The Lord our God has saved us."

22
It's the End of the World

Written for Pentecost during the beginning of the COVID-19 pandemic

MARK 13:5-8, 24-31

When I was a kid I was obsessed with the end of the world.

I wasn't looking forward to it or anything, nothing so macabre. You see, I didn't want the world to end, but there was something calming about being able to imagine life on the other side of it. It started out simple, with a couple of monster movies that showed the wreckage of the cities after Godzilla or King Ghidorah destroyed them. Seeing the survivors of these events, to me, they seemed strong. They would re-build, of that there was no doubt. Their faces were determined, as the set jaws of women and men and children alike left you knowing: they would stand on top of the wreckage as the monsters went back into the ocean ready to live again. That was the real part of the story that I wanted to emulate. To be a survivor. To be someone that could go through the end of the world and come out on the other side.

More recently I think that is the same attraction that our modern kids have to this run of graphic novels turned Netflix series. The title is "The Last Kids on Earth" and it is literally a child's fantasy story about living through the end of the world and being able to survive and thrive on the other side of that event. These kids are making all kinds of gadgets and weapons from spare bike parts. They make a defensible tree fort, and eat leftover preserved junk food anytime they want. Apparently, there is still something gratifying and attractive about seeing the story of a survivor.

These days I still like a good movie about an asteroid or a killer swarm of nano-bots taking over, but there are many more survival shows to choose from. I can get behind those usually and maybe fool myself into thinking that I really am learning a skill just in case things ever actually do go sour in this fragile thing called civilization. You know, just in case something really crazy happens, like a world-wide virus... or murder hornets.

There is something attractive to all of us in the notion of being a survivor. Even at the most basic level, part of the reason that the movie "Cast Away" did so well at the box office and world wide video release was the transformation and the determination that we as the audience were able to participate in as we watched this character on a deserted island. The movie, which if you haven't seen it, (spoilers!) is about a FedEx type executive who gets shipwrecked on an island outside of Fiji and lives there for years trying to make it back to civilization. In the movie, we lived through those days of struggle, finding water, making fire, and imagining the grueling defeat of never being able to make it over those waves. As he survives there is something in us that connects with the strength that it would take, and makes us feel strong too.

That's the attraction with the end of the world.

There is some sense, some hope, that on the other side of the end those who could survive would be the wise, the strong, the unbent of humanity.

Imagine then being a believer in the first century.

For many years the Christians lived in relative peace, though there were troubles immediately, as time went on that the eye of Rome turned toward them more fiercely and started finding reasons to kill them. Imagine being a Christian in this century living in places where being a Christian is against the law, or at the very least past the local tolerance limits of social design. Making it unpopular or dangerous to profess your belief. There are survivor stories there as well, as people make it through the end of their world. The end of their livelihoods. The end of their relationships. The end of their connections to the community.

There are many ways for our worlds to end.

We usually call that an apocalypse.

Even that word, meaning the end of everything, has a really crazy origin story. It is one of those words that has come to mean something so radically different from its origin that it is almost unrecognizable as a similar concept. This meaning, as the end of something, comes from a bad reading of the Book of Revelation. In the middling centuries where the church wanted to rule and create wealth through fear, the idea that creation would end in fiery death and destruction through beasts that roamed the earth made for great theater that missed the literary nature of the book of John's Revelation being a metaphor for the period in which it was written about the current era of the church. It was never meant to be a foretelling of a certain far flung future, but commentary on what was currently happening and the immediacy of God's Kingdom. The word *apakalypse* is from a Greek word meaning to "uncover" or "reveal." In Revelation, John was revealing the truth about what God's Kingdom was and would be. The style in which he wrote was that of an "uncovering truth". The same as the book of Daniel, and the same as the book of Mark.

I realize that a text from Mark might be a strange reading for a Sunday meant to celebrate the "birth" day of the church. We think we should be focused on the story of the disciples and followers who were driven out to spread Good News in the language of every person on earth. We should celebrate the nature of God's love and the Word that cannot be contained to one place, or one language, or one culture. It comes to every person as they are, tuned to their ear, and their dialect. Meaningful to their individual hearts. That's what Pentecost is after all.

Yet, that day, that Pentecost Day, was an apocalypse in both senses of the word. In the original Greek, yes, it was a *revelation*. It was a revelation to the followers of Christ who had the doors barred and locked, and it was a revelation to the people who were outside, a message so fervent and amazing and full of exuberance and joy that people thought they were drunk! They declared reality, they uncovered truth, they shouted out about the wonders of God. Also, in our modern understanding of 'apocalypse,' it was an ending of the world. The old world, the old understanding, the old methodologies and cultural norms that had ruled Israel, and Egypt, and Libya and Rome, and Asia, and Pontius -- those were over. Nothing would be the same after this. The movement called 'Christian Church' was taking hold, and on that first day three-thousand people never went back to their old lives. The nations eventually buckled and crumbled under the weight of this movement, and nothing would ever really stand against it. Not the Roman empire, not the decades of corruption within the church, not the evils of slavery and empire, or the call for war at any cost... the old world had died in a Firey Apocalypse on that day of Pentecost. The fire came down from Heaven and ate up the old world. Who would survive?

In this passage from Mark, we are reading Jesus' words of Apocalypse. The disciples want to know how they can survive. They know the end is coming, and they need Jesus to describe it to them so that they will be able to build a root cellar, or learn how to fish with their trousers, and start a fire with a bow drill. They ask Jesus, "Tell us how to prepare for the end of the world!"

Jesus first tells them to watch out. Because he knows that in our human nervousness, in our need to be among the survivors of the end, we are prone to believe people who lie. People who will tell us what we want to hear. Liars who make us comfortable. Charlatans who can hold a rally and get a raucous cheer. "Be wary of those people," the real Lord of Truth says. "Watch out for those who only *say* that they come in the name of Christ."

Then Jesus tells a story.

It's not a happy story or a funny parable.

It sounds like a terrible story. It sounds a lot like things we could nail down in our modern era, and people throughout history have done just that. Saying that this war, or this eclipse, or this earthquake was the one specifically mentioned. That this time we figured it out, and that Jesus is coming back with great power and glory. We are wrong of course. Yet we believe the human liars who tell us that this time it is different, because we all want to be among the survivors.

Jesus' message is a literal one and also a metaphoric one. A message not only to his followers, but to the early church, and to the modern church, and to all of the faithful for all time: Watch out. Be alert. Not anxiously, but aware. Awake in our spirits.

There are many ends to the world.

There is a final end to our mortal lives.

The sky and the earth will pass away someday as the sun expands billions and billions of years from now, but my Word will never end.

It is a message of hope, if we can hear it. It *is* a metaphor, but not only that, because the world *did* end on Pentecost. It ended on the day Jerusalem burned to the ground. It ended when Luther had enough of the errant Catholic structure. It ended when slaves and native americans died by the millions. It ended when the holocost murdered children. It ended when our students were killed at their schools in Newtown, Connecticut or in Parkland, Florida. The world has ended. The world will end. But the Word will not.

When the world is ending, in big ways or small ways, we all want to be part of that group that survives. And we are! In Christ's Grace, our old world ended, and with the advent of Pentecost the old way of doing things fell apart as the survivors of that heaven-shaking event were driven out to tell the story of the Gospel.

What better news could survivors bring?

We are called to bear witness to the transformation and the determination of our faith that has rested on us in the name of the Holy Spirit as blessed survivors of the wonderful end of the world.

As survivors, what is left but for us to emulate Jesus, to tell others how we survived, and to remind everyone to be wary.

Because, you see, the end of the world is coming.

23
The Journey after the Wreck

Written as the monuments of confederate generals were torn down

DANIEL 2:27-35

Reading the apocalyptic style of Daniel we might be able to write our own scriptural narrative based on current events here in the south. Imagine formulating news articles into archaic scrolls and ancient verbiage.

"Statues of bronze being toppled from their stonework bases, ignited in fire and drug into the waters." We don't have to dream about it, only walk outside our doors and see it for ourselves. The name of Columbus painted over with tags that condemn him. The work of some artist, now revealed as harmful. As we look again to this passage of Daniel, we perhaps resonate with the King's dream as we read the names of those long dead and reconsider their status.

Names were important in the ancient world. Nebuchadnezzar's very name is a prayer to the God Nabu, a god of wisdom and writing, to protect this person as a son. Nabu was also a son of Marduk, so the name makes sense for this Babylonian King. Daniel's Hebrew name was changed to Belteshazzar which also makes sense: it literally is a command to protect the life of the king. Names are like a story, or an important part of one, as we craft a narrative.

The Babylonians were intent on creating a new story for the Jewish people. As Isrealites had been pulled from their own countries to serve as slaves for the ruling class in distant Babylon, their new names were meant to reflect the authority of their masters. Hananiah, Mishael, and Azariah -- their names were also changed to tell stories about the gods of Babylon.

I realized this week that's how I felt about Columbus.

That I had been fed a different story. A narrative built around the name.

I used to really like Columbus. We shared a first name after all. As a kid, the narrative that I was fed was the one about this intrepid explorer. Who against all odds, doggedly went after his dream of exploration and sought patronage from the royals of Spain. Taking three ships! Imagine three ships! And sailing into the uncharted waters of the world. His slight gaff at missing the lands of India was forgiven in his discovery of a fantastic new world, setting up a trade line that altered the course of history. I love the exploration angle and the idea to never give up on your dreams. Somehow, in 1492, he sailed to prove the world was round... even though that was the same year that the globe was invented.

But that was a story. A made up story.

Made up by Washington Irving. An international author at the time, he published the biggest seller in American history that was seen through-out the western world. Irving wasn't a historian. He was a fiction writer. Sleepy Hollow, Rip Van Winkle, and the Knickerbocker Tales were his prior claims to fame, and yet, the story I heard of Columbus' life came from him. As truth. Even though we have Columbus' own journals. Even though we know the real story.

From letters and the journals we know that the royalty of Spain gave Columbus the bare minimum of ships to survive a journey across the ocean. Only the Santa Maria was large enough to be a cargo ship, the other two, a speedy caraval class, barely had room for the crew. It was a sign that they didn't have faith in Columbus. That they basically were trying to get rid of him. That his proposal was met with eye-rolling.

The Santa Maria was wrecked when they finally made landfall in what are now the Bahaman Islands. The local natives, the Lucayans, fed and cared for the crew and repaired the ship. From the kindness of the natives, Columbus wrote about their weakness. Seeing their gold, and noting how easy they would be to enslave, he returned to visit genocide on them in a search for their precious metals. He went back to Europe, creating his own fiction well enough to complete a new company based on his lies and greed.

From his own hand we know that when Columbus returned in force he created horror by having his men cut off the ears and hands of the idegeounous people and forcing the Lucayans to wear them around their necks to control them by the starkness of their malignant hate. Rewarding the evil of his own crew with pre-flowered girls from the tribal community. The historian in me reads the kinds of things Columbus did and wonders how different he was from his contemporaries, but the reality is that I do not appreciate sharing his name anymore.

And that feels like a loss, but I would rather know the truth.

This was not an intrepid explorer. This was an opportunist looking for wealth and willing to do evil things in order to get it.

The King of Babylon was the "ruler of the world."

The authoritative power he wielded was over everything.

People did what he said. You had your name changed to serve him. Slaves were for his bidding. If there was news he didn't like, any lie he created became the new truth. Crowds surrounded his palace calling for his deification. Anyone who questioned his bizarre and insane will was ostracized or killed as a traitor to their country.

But that's not the real story.

The King has a dream of the real story. A babylonian statue. A fine figure. A dashing image made of all the precious metals of the earth. Carved and beautiful as it stands in the sun. It is dazzling and awesome! But that isn't the real story. Because then, a stone, a simple stone, made of unimpressive rock, destroys this finely carved work of art. And the king laments. He wrings his hands and wails. He is so distraught that he can't even talk about the dream to the people that he wants to interpret it. The whole first part of this chapter is a back and forth with the best and the brightest of Babylon. The king says, "explain my dream" and the astrologers say, "of course tell us what you saw in the dream" and the king says "no, tell me about it first." What?! The astrologers give up and are about to be put to death when Daniel intercedes.

Not every form of apocalyptic literature is so forthcoming with the meaning of its imagery. Daniel has many places where the dreams that are meant to be revelations are explicitly explained, in the same way Jesus sometimes does in the gospels, explaining a parable in detail after he tells it.

Here, Daniel tells the real story.

God's kingdom is greater. Greater than this kingdom, Nebuchadnezzar, greater than you and the dynasty that comes after you and the one that comes after that and on and on. It doesn't matter how many kingdoms come, whether they are divided or unified, God will not only destroy and replace them, but grow greater than them. That's the truth.

For the king and his people, for all they have achieved. For all the culture and scientific progress they have made there is a loss in this revelation. In this apocalypse.

The king throws himself down. A good response. We might expect the King to double down, to get rid of Daniel or to at least say, "no, wrong, that wasn't my dream." But the dream has shaken him so much, and the truth comes as such a relief, that he folds up and lays down in front of Daniel.

An unheard of thing for a king to do. Perhaps we can relate. Imagine everything you thought you knew about your kingdom, your life, your work, and realizing that it was meant to be destroyed and replaced.

One of the many gifts that my dad has given me over the years is a love for science-fiction. It has literally shaped the way that I interact with the world, and from an early age watched GORT the robot from "The Day the Earth Stood Still" with nail biting eagerness. The thing we probably watched the most was Star Trek the Next Generation. This wonderful legacy to Gene Rodenberry's original groundbreaking work made a habit of looking at everything humanity was and imagining what they could be at their best. There is one episode that I remembered especially when looking at the text this week. An episode in which Lt. Commander Data, the resident Android and operations officer, builds another android daughter and names her Lal, who's name is Hindi for "beloved." He spends much of the episode teaching her and talking philosophy and in one such scene they are talking about Data's insistence on trying to emulate human emotion even though he lacks the basic programming to do so. Lal asks, "What purpose does emulating emotion serve, except to remind you that you are incomplete?"

I wonder if this is why we as humans can back off from our own truths? Because they are painful.

It *is* sad to tear down a hero of childhood, even when the truth is that they were harmful and murderous. They become a reminder that we are incomplete, or broken, and so we retreat back to the safety of a narrative created by Washington Irving instead. The truth becomes too much. Too real. Too terrible. That's what Nebuchadnezzar does. After hearing the truth, he retreats back into his lie. The first thing he does in the next chapter is make a Golden Statue of himself. Daring God to knock it down.

In the episode of Star Trek, Lt. Commander Data responds to his daughter's question. He comments that it is a struggle to be more than he was taught to be. He notes that it is the struggle that is most important. He says to her, "We must strive to be more than we are, it does not matter that we will not reach our goal, the effort is it's own reward."

Statues are being torn down.

Maybe the reality of the history that they represent is hard for us. Maybe it was someone we once revered as a child. Maybe we feel the loss of that false narrative and what it meant, but if we are really the people of God, the dreamers known by our *real* names, then we have to own that struggle.

It's possible we will never achieve the utopian society of God's true Kingdom until Christ returns, but it is the struggle, the journey, the *effort* that is the most important part. It is through that effort that the good works of Christ are made known to the world. Remember that the coming of the 'Mountain,' the rock that destroys the rulership of the empire, is not something made by human hands. Daniel says that in verse 45 of chapter 2. Our work is to angle toward the mountain, but the reality of it is God's alone.

We are meant to see and live in the truth.

To see that the gold and silver and bronze statuary of our fallen kingdoms are meant to be crushed by God's new reality.

We are meant to live in that, and even if we have limitations in our programming, we are meant for the effort to be better, to listen better, to love better knowing that there is no "goal" to achieve. Only the journey toward the mountain.

Let's continue this journey together.

24
In the Time of Wrath

Written after the death of Representative John Lewis

DANIEL 8:17-26

In chapter 8 of the book Daniel we begin a new section of visions.

If we aren't careful with how we read them it's possible that we could become a little 'lost in the weeds' on the repetition of visions and time tables and explanations. It is important to keep in mind a few things.

One is that the book of Daniel is an apocalyptic work of literature.

That means that the style it is written in is intended to bring a new revelation to people, it is intended to bring a great light and to be a book that gives people hope above all else. The writings are intended to speak to an ancient audience as well as a modern one, so we don't necessarily need to spend our time trying to figure out the numbers of when these visions came to pass or will come to pass in the future. Also, chapter 8 begins the Hebrew section of the book of Daniel. The first few books, aside from chapter 1, were written in Aramaic, which made the story of Daniel and the visions of various kings (which contain the more famous parts of the story) their own set of adventures within this larger book. The use of Aramaic also highlights the importance of these stories as something that is built more for the unbeliever, as Aramaic was widely used in the ancient empires. So we can consider chapters 2-7 a message built for the people of the empire to hear, and not just a message for the Jewish people (which may explain why Hannaiah, Azaria and Mishael are referred to through their Babylonian names). This makes sense because as we read chapters 2-7 we can see how they could be used as an ancient proselytization tool. One that would be helpful in convincing the people of the ancient world that the wise emperors humbled themselves before God and the foolish ones were doomed to fail as they chose arrogant narcissism instead.

This means that in chapter 8, as we return to a portion of the book that was written in Hebrew, we are in essence returning to a part of the book that is intended more for the Jewish people, or the believers who already knew God.

Which doesn't mean it is any easier to understand.

Chapter 8 seems like a repeat of the vision that Daniel had in chapter 7. There are horns and beasts -- in this case a ram and a goat -- which we are told represents the kingdoms of the Medo-Persians and of Greece. This chapter also talks about the spread of power that these empires and the leader of the last empire in this section exalt in themselves. So, there is a sense that political power gives way to a religious power or a support of the religious powers.

There is a question that is repeated throughout the book of Daniel, the question of "how long?" Daniel, throughout the years that these visions take place Daniel will ask this question: "How long?" How long until the Lord's power is known? How long until the followers of God experience true freedom. How long until the evil of the world finally is broken?

That's a question many of us have been asking as well. How long does this COVID-19 virus last? How long do we have to maintain this alternative way of living? How long will the effects of the virus continue?

The cry of how long is deep in our human condition. Throughout scripture, not just in Daniel. In Psalm 13 it laments that God has forgotten the author. That the writer of this psalm is being overcome by the enemy, and is wrestling with their thoughts with a deep sorrow in their heart. Psalm 13 isn't very long, but it is very powerful. The cry of 'How Long?' is a valid one.

Famously, the cry of 'How Long?' is also a cry heard through the Civil Rights Movement, both in the 1960s and today. Rev Dr Martin Luther King gave an address on the steps of the Capitol in Montgomery Alabama that repeated the refrain. He asks: "How long will it take? How long will prejudice blind the visions... and darken understanding? How long will justice be crucified and truth bear it?"

Perhaps we are asking those same questions still. How long will we keep hearing of another unarmed person of color who is killed in their beds' asleep. Of another person who is killed because of mistaken identity, or the color of their skin. Of another person who is beaten because they dare question our problematic and harmful systems. We still ask 'How long?' It can be depressing and painful to feel trapped in the asking of that question with no answer.

Last Friday, on the 17th, one of my personal heroes passed away. I had the honor of meeting John Lewis at a reception in Washington. It was after a few friends and I had been demonstrating and participating in an action with 'Bread for The World,' a christian policy activist group that seeks to simply feed people. There was some legislation coming up at the time that would expand how WIC was used to buy things fresh at farmers' markets and a few other action points we wanted to make come to life for our legislators. So, we were part of a group of thousands that arrived that day in D.C.

Honestly, I can't remember how our small group of friends got invited to the reception, but somehow we were there, and then, so was John Lewis who came to thank us for the work we had done for Food Justice that day. I was embarrassed because I was wearing what an outdoor protestor should wear in the summer months of northern Virginia; shorts and a t-shirt, and I felt brutally underdressed. But, my friends encouraged me, and I am glad they did, because not only did John pose for a photo with me, shorts and all, but also spoke to me about the work he saw us doing and the "fire he saw in my eyes." I was blessed and inspired by his kindness and genuine spirit.

John Lewis grew up picking cotton with his family, who's mother would get them up early while the dew was still sitting heavy on the cotton to pick as much as they could for the day. He grew up during the heat of the Civil Rights movement and marched arm in arm with Rev. Dr. King. He said that the work he did for justice was a "fire burning up in your bones and you cannot be silent." Coming from a man who was beaten almost to death by members of the Klu Klux Klan -- more than once -- his outlook always gave me courage to find my voice and to find the thing in my life that was a fire in my bones.

When I think of John, I think of the angel Gabriel coming to Daniel. In our reading today, the angel Gabriel (who's name means "God is my Strength") tells Daniel, "You are only human..." It is taxing for the "only human" in us to absorb the story of the apocalypse.

Our spirits might be getting tired, and feeling a lot like the author of Psalm 13; feeling those sleepless nights and sorrow filled hearts, asking God to return light to our eyes.

Gabriel says something else to Daniel as well; even though Daniel is only human he still needs to understand.

Daniel is only human but there is a fire in his bones.

Daniel is only human, but the book bears his name and is meant to bring hope to a nation in pain.

John Lewis tells a story about hope that he found early in life through a message that Rev. Dr. King spoke about a lot. He would say that "one day, they are going to tell a story about a group of people... and the world that they changed." In an interview John remembers this story and says that without this message, without this hope in his life, he doesn't know what would have happened to him. He says, "I would have been lost."

Prophets, church leaders, our spiritual support systems, these "only human" people of our lives are important as they give us hope when we cry out the lament of Psalm 13, "How long God?"

When the rulers and the government in this chapter of Daniel have become as evil as possible: when the rulers think they are great; when the rulers kill many people; when the rulers attack the people of God. We cry out, "how long?"

When we reflect on the powerful faith of the Civil Rights Movement of the 60's and still look to see the deep divides against justice today, we might take that cry up again; "how long?"

In the middle of a pandemic where numbers still seem to be rising during a time when things were supposed to be getting better.

In a time where cities across the country continue to demonstrate and protest the injustice of our systems, when that work was supposed to have been improved we can wearily repeat the phrase, "how long?"

In Daniel 8, I am glad we have returned to Hebrew because there is this great Hebrew word. It is used in verse 25 in which the angel (God's Strength) gives a message meant to strengthen Daniel and the people: no matter how great the leader thinks they are, God will crush them. That awesome Hebrew word is "sha-vair." Which sounds like "shatter" in some way and means similarly "to be crushed into pieces." To be ripped apart. To be ruptured, broken and torn down. Which doesn't lend itself to the strength Gabriel is trying to bring, but as we are watching statues fall on the news or in person we might have an idea what that would look like and feel like. Yet, there are other ways for something to be shattered.

John Lewis tells a story about one of those Klannsmen that nearly beat him to death.

It was so many years later when John had his office in Washington as a representative in the House from Georgia, when he had an unscheduled visitor. A man, from Georgia and his young son, came into his office. And explained why they were there. This man revealed himself as one of the men who beat John, and in contrite and heartfelt humility, he asked for John's forgiveness for his actions and his vile beliefs.

John could have had him thrown out. He could have had congressional security throw him out or even arrest him. He could have told his son how badly he was beaten by his father and the rank evil that his father followed. But, John was better than someone who would misuse his authority and forcefully remove this man and his son. He was better than someone who would let old anger and pain dictate his actions.

Instead, John reached out and embraced the man.

Held this man who had beaten him in hate.

The man, his son and John broke down in tears.

"Sha-vair."

There are many ways that God can break things.

Did all the members of the Ku Klux Klan come asking John's forgiveness? No. Some are broken in reconciliation and some have yet to be broken down and destroyed in other ways. Still on the other side of repentance and remorse, there can be an awesome beauty.

Rev. Dr. King, in that address from 1957, not only asks but answers the question of "How Long?" He says "Not long, because no lie can live forever. *Not long*, because you reap what you sow; *not long*, because the arc of the moral universe bends toward justice; *not long*, because God's truth is marching on."

Psalm 13 says, "*Not long*, because of the trust we have in the unfailing Love of God."

Daniel says, "*Not long*, because God is the supreme ruler of all and God will break authority built on lies and governments made on harm."

Not long sometimes still seems like too long, but the 60's have another lesson for us. A theology that was repeated as they struggled to effect change, in the same ways we struggle now. The idea that there is a better day, a new day, coming but that new day needs our help.

We have to create a way out of no way.

I think of that when I feel like evil has a hold of us, when it seems like things will never be normal again.

We are creating the way.

Our engagement, our action, our service. Our fire.

If we can find the fire that God has placed in our bones, then our spirits will not be silent when looking to that new day. Daniel is disturbed by his dream, yet the fire God put in him, to bring hope to his people and to us, still stands.

The truth of the world, the moral arc of the universe, the reality of God is this: that selfishness, hubris, and hate have no purpose in creation, and they will be destroyed by a group of people that changed the world.

By people who made a way.

By people with a fire in their bones who answer the question of how long, with that hopeful glorious response -- *not long now*.

www.ingramcontent.com/pod-product-compliance
Lightning Source LLC
Chambersburg PA
CBHW071455070526
44578CB00001B/350